WALKING TO MAINE

A SCOUTMASTER'S JOURNEY ON

THE APPALACHIAN TRAIL

GLENN JUSTIS

This book is for Laine and Joe. Of all the rocks I encountered on the trail, none were as strong as you.

The wolf on the hill is never as hungry as the wolf climbing the hill -
Fearless Motivation

TABLE OF CONTENTS

FOREWORD

"You want to do what?" This was my reaction when my husband brought up the idea of thru-hiking the Appalachian Trail. We had been together for 30 years at the time and I knew him well, so it didn't really surprise me that he wanted to do this. He was working as a Prosecuting Attorney and was coming to a point in his career where he needed a change. After 11 years of dealing with criminals and politics, it was time. A change I'm not sure he would have made if not for taking time for himself and hiking the AT. He had given so much of himself to everyone else for so many years, and it was now his time to do for himself and take a break. He deserved this adventure and as much as our son and myself would miss him, it would only make us stronger.

He loves the outdoors and as a Scoutmaster to Boy Scout Troop 2 in Summerville, SC, he had spent a lot of time outdoors and hiking. He had taught the scouts to always reach for the big dreams. "Go big or go home!" He teaches us all how living simply in the woods can change you and help you to understand that you can be happy without all of the "extras" in life.

In this book, Glenn Justis, aka Scoutmaster, shows his scouts and others what it means to follow your dreams. He tells stories of his adventures and how his faith in humanity is restored. He shares stories of the hikers he met along the trail and also of the "trail angels" who helped support him. It is amazing how people who don't know you will come out and help you and it always seemed to come at the exact time he needed it. Even as a spouse at home, I found comfort in the "trail angels" who reached out to me and gave me support as well.

Times were not always easy on the trail or at home. Rain, snow and a tragedy at home would hit but the trail would provide a way for him to persevere and reach his goal.

Scoutmaster brings it all to life in this book about his five-month walk to Maine.

Laine Justis

"Mrs. Scoutmaster"

CHAPTER 1

The Trail Beckons

I can remember the moment I got the phone call. It was my mother on the other end and she informed me that my Dad was being taken by ambulance to the hospital. I was walking back to my office after grabbing some lunch and I quickly went to my desk, grabbed my car keys and told my coworkers my Dad had a heart attack and I needed to go. It was Thursday, May 4, 2012, and I had just eaten dinner with my parents the night before.

Up to that point, things were going well in my life. I was a Criminal Prosecutor and my wife, Laine, was a Registered Nurse. Our son, Joe, was in the 5th grade and was about to finish elementary school and move on to middle school. I had recently started a new Boy Scout troop in town and served as the Scoutmaster. My parents, both retired and in their late 70s, split time with us in South Carolina and with my two older brothers and their families in New Jersey and Pennsylvania.

Over the next eight months, our family would experience my father suffering a massive heart attack only to return home four days later and suffer a massive stroke the next morning. He hung on for three months before passing away in August. During his time in the hospital and nursing home, my mother was diagnosed with bladder cancer and underwent a radical cystectomy barely a month after my Dad's funeral. She lasted only four more months before passing away in January 2013.

Losing a parent is never easy. Losing both just five months apart makes you wonder what else could go wrong. As each holiday and birthday arrives, you celebrate it but also acknowledge their passing. Over time, the hurt subsides but it never goes away. I took comfort in the fact that they lived long lives, had each other, had a good family, and were active up until their final sicknesses.

After my Mom passed, I spent most of my free time working with the Boy Scout troop. Along with some other parents that I had been with for five years in Cub Scouts, we built the troop into a strong group and were able to provide fun and adventure for the boys. Both my Mom and my Dad were active as leaders when I was a scout. They loved Scouting and I knew they were happy that I was involved again with my son, Joe.

When we were putting the troop together, I spoke with my Cub Scouts and informed them that we were going to start a new Boy Scout troop. I explained all the fun and cool things we could do as Boy Scouts. I asked them, "If you could go anywhere, do anything, what would it be?" A small hand shot up in the air and I pointed to Cotter, who was 10 years old. "The Grand Canyon," he said with a smile. I immediately responded with "alright, we will go there," but then quickly added, "it won't be right away, it may take a few years but we will get there."

Starting a new Boy Scout troop is not an easy thing to do. We had no money and no equipment but we did have some motivated adults and a group of kids that just wanted to have fun and had not been ruined by the normal limitations that parents so often put on their kids. Instead of telling them "we can't do that" when they came up with a suggestion for a campout or event, we would ask, "how can we do that?". We started doing bigger and better things. We pushed ourselves beyond what we thought we were capable of doing. We were not only teaching the kids to think big and reach for lofty goals, but the adults were also starting to think we could do some incredible things.

With each goal we accomplished, we would try to think of something even bigger to achieve the next time.

Without a lot of money and equipment, we had to focus on doing more with less. I taught the scouts to get a backpack and start acquiring their gear. We incorporated hiking into our outings because it allowed us to camp in more remote areas and see and do things other troops were not doing. We were Troop 2 The Deuce, and we did fun stuff. As we hiked more, I could see the improvement in our camping and backpacking skills. We even completed a 50-mile hike over Christmas break in 2013. It was the greatest scouting trip I had ever done up to that point. The average age of the scouts was 12 years old but they carried full packs and completed the trek.

By now, the hiking bug had spread and we were known as a high adventure troop. While other troops were still doing the usual car camping and cookie cutter Council campouts, Troop 2 sought and created their own adventure. It was a culture we developed in the troop and we did not apologize for it. We were going back to Scouting's roots and putting the "outing" in Scouting.

By the summer of 2014, we had been talking about the Grand Canyon trip for nearly 2 1/2 years and the time to put up or shut up was upon us. I decided to set the date for Spring Break 2015 and announced it to the troop. The plan was not only to visit the Grand Canyon but actually hike all the way to the bottom and back up again. We eventually applied and were approved for a backcountry permit that allowed us to take nine scouts and do a 3-day, 2-night hike in the Canyon. One of the scouts going on the trip was 13-year-old Cotter. His idea was coming to fruition.

As I sat in the terminal at the Charleston Airport, waiting to board a plane to carry Troop 2 westward, I walked over to the Hudson News stand and browsed the bookstand. I was looking to see if any books caught my attention and would make for good reading on the long flight to Arizona. I immediately spotted a book called "Hiking Through" and picked up the book to learn more. It was a book about one man's journey on the Appalachian Trail after his wife died from cancer. Since I was about to embark on a hiking trip out west, I thought it might be a good book to put me in a hiking state of mind.

While I had heard of the Appalachian Trail, I had only been on it once, a one-mile section in New Jersey the summer before when my troop spent a week at Camp NoBeBoSco, a Boy Scout camp in Blairstown, NJ. The camp is best known as the filming location of the original 1980s movie, Friday the 13th. While reading the book, I was introduced not only to some of the history and details of the trail, but also some of its lore and traditions.

Stretching nearly 2,200 miles from Georgia to Maine, the Appalachian Trail traverses some of the oldest mountains in the world and is the longest hiking-only trail in the world. The trail was the vision of a man named Benton McKaye, and with help from Myron Avery and thousands of volunteers, the footpath was completed in 1937. A person who walks the entire length of the trail in a year's time is known as a thru-hiker while those who hike only parts or "sections" of the trail are called section hikers. The trail is maintained by several dozen volunteer hiking clubs that stretch the entire length.

In 1948, a World War II veteran named Earl Schaffer became the first person to hike the entire length in one year. He used his time on the trail as a form of self-therapy to "walk off the war". Several years later, Emma "Grandma" Gatewood became the first female to solo hike the trail. Most of the hikers are younger men and women, retirees, or those in between careers.

The trail is managed by the Appalachian Trail Conservancy

or ATC and they maintain statistics regarding successful thru-hike attempts and act as an advocacy group for the trail. Over the last couple of decades, the popularity of the trail has increased and over 3,000,000 people hike at least a portion of the trail every year. Even though between 3,000-4,000 hikers attempt a thru-hike each year, the success rate is between 20-25%.

The trail is marked with approximately 83,000 white blazes, a 2-inch by 6-inch strip of white paint affixed to trees, rocks, overpasses, and the like. These white blazes act as a road map to hikers and blaze the trail from Springer Mountain, GA to Mt. Katahdin, ME. A hiker must traverse approximately 5 million footsteps and carry everything he or she needs to survive on their back. Through rain, snow, sleet, sun, heat, and cold, the hiker pushes forward in pursuit of the finish line.

As I read more and more of the book, I became intrigued by the trail. While I was about to embark on a short three-day hike, it wasn't the actual hiking that was so intriguing but the adventure of getting away from the busy day to day rat race and being out in nature. The feeling of being self-sufficient and not knowing what sights and sounds you would experience each day were part of the allure of the adventure. For me, the Grand Canyon was sure to provide some of the most beautiful views a person would see in their lifetime and would also allow a person to see nature's beauty and appreciate God's creation.

I saw the same type of feeling being described in the book about the AT, and my excitement grew as we traveled west. When we finally arrived at the Grand Canyon and prepared to see and hike it for the first time, it did not disappoint. The reaction of the scouts and my own reaction was one of pure awe and amazement. As I sat on the ground at Plateau Point in the middle of the Canyon, I thought back to the talk I had with my Cub Scouts about the troop we were creating and the adventures we said we would experience.

As I sat there and took it all in, one of my Assistant Scoutmasters walked over and simply said, "Good job, Scoutmaster." I thought about how far we had come as a troop. I looked at the scouts as they posed for pictures and thought about the first camping trips they took as young Cub Scouts and remembered the very first hike I took them on, a one-mile walk into the woods. Halfway through, they started to ask how much longer there was to hike. I responded over and over again with, "not far, we are almost there, just keep hiking." I looked at them now and here they were in the Grand Canyon. We were living proof that consistent action towards a goal will yield incredible results.

While flying back to South Carolina, I dove back into the book with a new sense of adventure. Our troop had just had the most incredible experience and I knew I wanted more. I arrived home late in the evening and went to sleep. The next day, I went to the mailbox to get the mail and as I sorted through it, I came across a letter from the Appalachian Trail Conservancy. It was a solicitation for a donation to the ATC and I found it strange that I received it when I did. I had never received anything from them before and it was very coincidental that I got it right after returning from a Grand Canyon trip and right after starting to read my first AT book. It was as if somebody was trying to tell me something.

I knew we needed to bring the rest of the troop back to the Canyon and got more and more interested in hiking and ultra-light backpacking. While researching light-weight gear and backcountry cooking options and methods, I came across some hiking videos on YouTube and decided to see what gear AT thru-hikers used. I figured if anyone knew what to use, it would be someone hiking 2,200 continuous miles. As I watched as part of my research to gather information for my scouts, I noticed something else was happening, I was becoming more and more intrigued by the idea of hiking the AT.

I watched AT videos on YouTube and started to follow thru-hikers who recorded their trek as they hiked, and I started to not only pull for them to accomplish their dream, but I began to envy them. I found myself thinking more and more about the trail and knew that I would want to do it if I ever got the chance. Maybe one day after Joe was out of college and out of the house after I retired and saved a good nest egg. The only problem was, would I be healthy enough to do it then? Would I even live that long?

I had spent the last decade prosecuting murderers, robbers, rapists, and all sorts of criminals. I enjoyed what I did and loved being able to help crime victims. Since being a lawyer was a second career for me and I was happy being a Prosecutor, I really did not have any plans on leaving the office in pursuit of more money or other opportunities. Most prosecutors serve in the position for a few years, just long enough to get some experience, then leave for greener pastures. I never had the desire to do that. But that was changing.

I often wondered whether or not I would enjoy having my own law practice and working for myself rather than working for others. A big part of me did not want to leave my current job as I felt a tremendous amount of loyalty to it. At the same time, it was difficult to see others go out on their own and make their own way knowing that I could be in their shoes if I just took the plunge. Despite that, it was difficult to pull the trigger.

In addition, I also found myself wishing I could hike the AT sooner rather than later. Each time I would think about it, my mind would tell me all the reasons I could not do it at that time. Family obligations, financial obligations, and other excuses constantly flooded my brain when I tried to think about when I could do it. I also felt a tremendous amount of loyalty to my job and my employer. Finally, something changed. Instead of asking myself why I could not hike the trail sooner rather than later, I asked myself how I could hike the trail sooner rather than later. That simple distinction made all the difference in the world.

As soon as I changed the question, the answers started to change. Our brains naturally want to solve problems. By asking how, my brain got busy finding answers to the question. I was able to figure out how to afford not only hiking the trail, but how to survive without an income during the hike and still pay the bills that would need to be paid. I figured out the best time of the year for me to start the trail and whether to travel north or south. What would Laine do? What about Joe? What about my job? All these questions were addressed. More importantly, I asked myself what would happen if I did not do the trail. I realized I was not getting any younger and I needed to do it while I was still healthy and did not have any nagging injuries.

I had spent the last several years preaching to my scouts that they should dream big and take risks in life. It was time for me to follow my own advice. Like a true lawyer, I prepared my argument and brought up the topic with Laine. I laid out why I thought it would be beneficial to us for me to hike the trail and why now was the right time. To my surprise, she said ok. I didn't know if she really wanted me to do it or she was just being nice. I didn't ask twice. I took her answer and ran with it.

It was June 2017 and I went into work the next day and told a coworker I was planning on hiking the trail next year. When asked what I was going to do about my job, I told her that I didn't know but I would figure it out. I had permission from the two people that mattered (Laine and Joe) and that was good enough for me.

I knew this was a big decision and the usual doubt would attempt to creep into my brain. When it did, I would remind myself of how this adventure could be a way to allow me to turn a new page and be a better husband, father, and overall a better person. I knew deep down that change was not going to come by doing what I was doing and a change in scenery was needed.

That evening, I was about to go to bed when I received a call from a cousin who informed me that one of my brothers was in the hospital. He was in ICU on a ventilator and things did not look good. He was only 54 years old and was an EMT and volunteer firefighter. He hadn't felt good for about a week and finally relented and went to the ER after his shift and immediately coded. After 45 minutes of CPR, the medical team finally got his heart started again but he never regained consciousness. Less than 48 hours later, my other brother, Joe, and myself stood at his bedside as he took his last breath.

As Joe and I waited in line at the Lehigh Valley Airport car rental desk, a girl wearing a pair of Crocs with socks was in line. She had a backpack on with a pair of boots hanging from it and trekking poles collapsed and stuck in the side pocket. I knew the Appalachian Trail was not too far away and with it being June 17th, she had to be a northbound thru-hiker.

I approached her and asked if she was thru-hiking. She told me she was and had completed around 1,300 miles. She had a family emergency and had to rent a car to drive home for a bit. I wished her luck and continued to the terminal. As I walked through the airport, I took that chance meeting with a thru-hiker as a sign that my decision to hike the trail was the right decision. Losing my brother at only 54 years old reinforced the fact that life is short and we are not guaranteed tomorrow. I never doubted my decision from that moment forward.

I started preparations as soon as I arrived home and began assembling the gear I would need. I decided to start on January 30th just a few days after my son's birthday. Leaving in January would mean I would hit winter in the south but would hopefully finish before the really hot weather up north and before it started to turn cold up north. I decided to video my trek and share it on YouTube for family and friends and whoever else might want to follow. Eventually, I announced my plans on social media and sat back and waited for the response.

As you might imagine, some people were super supportive and envious of my opportunity while others were supportive but glad they were not doing it. Finally, there were those that questioned the decision. At that point, I really did not care what people thought. The supporters gave me encouragement and the haters gave me motivation. A lot was on the line and there was no turning back. My job was going to allow me to take an unpaid leave of absence, so I worked extra hard to wrap up as many cases as I could before I left for the trail. I didn't want to leave my co-workers with a lot of extra work, so I did whatever I could to get stuff done.

As the days to my start date dwindled, I put the finishing touches on my gear and logistical planning. A week before leaving for the trail, I was called into the boss's office and was informed my employment had been terminated and my position would not be held for me. I would need to pack up my things and be gone by the end of the day. I was told I could re-apply when I got back but, for now, my services after 14 years were no longer needed.

As I packed up my office, I thought about the upcoming hike and about all the reasons I wanted to do the hike. Getting terminated a week before I was supposed to be leaving for the hike was the final sign that I was doing the right thing. It was actually a blessing. Now I had permission to go and did not have to feel any guilt for leaving my job. This was not going to be just another adventure. This was going to be something that would change my life. I believed deep in my heart that after hiking 2,200 miles and climbing mountains for 5 months, there would not be a chance in hell that I would return the same person. I was a free man and the trail was calling.

CHAPTER 2

Stepping Out

Morning came early as the alarm rang out. As I climbed out of bed and turned off the alarm, the feelings of excitement and apprehension pulsed through my body. I wiped the sleep from my eyes and headed to the bathroom. I stood under the warm shower and thought about the journey I was about to embark on. The hot shower water felt good as it warmed my body and helped to wake me. As I stood in the shower, I thought about the fact it would be days before I would shower again. As crazy as it seems, I tried to scrub extra hard knowing this shower would have to last me for a while. After drying off, I began the slow and methodical process of getting dressed. I put on the clothes I had carefully laid out the night before and began to eat a granola bar and take my vitamins.

I carefully double-checked my pack and made sure I had everything before hoisting it up and on my shoulders for what would be the first time of many. Joe helped me carry the bags out to the car, while Laine went to check out of the hotel. When I walked out of the hotel and into the darkness of the early morning, the cold air hit me in the face. It was a stark reminder that it was late January and I would be experiencing this type of weather quite a bit over the next several weeks and possibly months. After placing the bags in the car, I looked over my right shoulder to the east just as the sun was starting its ascent over the rolling mountains of North Georgia. The sky started to illuminate in a plethora of oranges and gold. As I shivered, I tried to block out the cold air that was cutting through my clothing and focus on the beauty of the moment. I stared at the mountains knowing that, in a few hours, I would be engulfed within them, making my way northbound to Maine. Whenever any thoughts of doubt would attempt to creep in, I would just tell myself that this was my world now. For the last six months, I had prepared for this moment and there was no turning back.

The ride up Springer started out fine but as the miles passed and we climbed higher and higher, the road conditions worsened and the temperature gauge started to drop. Frozen ruts and divots in the road made the drive difficult but we eventually reached the parking lot. As I sat in the car before getting out, I tried to savor the warmth of the vehicle. I knew it would be at least several days before I would be this warm again. The temperature gauge read 19 degrees but it felt much colder when I stepped out into the early morning mountain air and the wind began to sap whatever warmth was in my body and send cold chills down to my core. I thought to myself, "what the hell did you get yourself into, Glenn?" but was determined to deal with it and not waste the opportunity.

I found the white blaze that marked the trail next to the parking lot and Joe and I began the 1-mile climb to the Springer summit. It was a 400' climb but as the adrenaline was coursing through me, the climb did not seem to be bad. Joe and I chatted as we hiked and, before I knew it, we emerged from the woods to a small clearing. I looked down and saw the iconic plaque embedded into the stone base of the mountain. It would mark the starting line for my journey. A journey filled with expectation but also the unknown. I stared out from the summit and tried to take in the beauty of the view. The sky was clear, the sun was brightly shining, and the wind cut through the layers of clothing protecting my body. I made my way over to the rock that housed the logbook. Sliding open the metal draw that was built into the rock, I pulled out the ziplock bag containing the logbook. I gripped a pen in my gloved hand and recorded my presence at the southern terminus by inscribing "The wolf on the top of the hill is not as hungry as the wolf climbing the hill. Pushing north, Scoutmaster on the AT 2018." I paused for a moment for Joe to take my picture then he followed behind me as I took my first steps northward to Maine.

Joe and I chatted as we made our way back down to the parking lot where Laine and others waited for us. My adventure had officially begun and each step I took brought me closer to the end. As I hiked, my body warmed up and I started to get comfortable with the trail. In what seemed like no time at all, we appeared from the woods and could see the parking lot. Laine appeared from the car and prepared for the final goodbye. As long as I was moving, I was able to stay warm but standing there in the parking lot only made me shiver. Laine and I hugged and kissed, then said our goodbyes. Before leaving, I told her I loved her and would see her in a couple of weeks. I turned and headed towards the white blaze that was painted on the tree. I swallowed hard and kept my head looking forward as I continued north on the trail. When I walked far enough to be out of view of the parking lot, I looked back and took a deep breath. The trek had begun.

As I continued to walk, I began to take in the views around me. Despite the cold, it was a beautiful day and I was grateful for the sunny weather. While descending the mountain, I became engrossed in the woods and the wind died down to almost a non-existent whisper. I started to work up a slight sweat as the constant moving and the lack of wind allowed my body to produce the heat necessary to keep my body warm under the down puffer jacket I was wearing. Eventually, I stopped and removed my jacket then quickly threw my pack back onto my back and got moving again.

As I hiked throughout the day, I thought about Laine and Joe as they rode home together. I hoped that having each other there would help keep their spirits up and not make them too sad. I stopped by a dirt road crossing at Hickory Flats in order to eat some lunch. I had over 6 miles logged for the day and was feeling pretty good. I had to put my jacket back on to stay warm but took it back off before starting back on the trail after lunch. About an hour later, I passed the side trail leading to Hawk Mountain shelter. Since it wasn't even 1:30 pm, I pushed north and decided I would stop at Devil's Kitchen and camp there for the night. That would put me at mile marker 14.4 and with the 1-mile climb up to Springer, would give me solid first-day mileage. Since it was early in the season and a Tuesday, other hikers were scarce on the trail. As I neared the 14-mile mark, I began to check my Guthooks app to make sure I did not pass the campsite I was planning to stay at for the night. On cue at the 14.4 mark, I noticed off to the right of the trail the beginnings of a campfire and two hikers gathering wood to feed the newly lit fire they had created.

I said hello and scoped out a flat spot to set up my tent. After getting my tent set up, I grabbed my water bladder and trudged down to the creek that was nearby to gather some water before cooking dinner. It felt good to get the pack off my back and get set-up for my first-ever night on the AT. Filtering water, while not a difficult chore, was made uncomfortable as the water was ice cold and it did not take long for my hands and fingers begin to freeze from the cold water and cold January air. As I poured some water into my cooking pot and started to boil it for my ramen and tuna, I observed the small plastic bottle of olive oil I packed was frozen to the point that the oil was congealed and thick. As my meal finished cooking, I grabbed the pot in my gloved hands and savored the heat as it began to thaw out my hands and fingers which were still frozen from filtering my water.

After dinner and cleaning my pot, I approached the other hikers and introduced myself. They were doing a multi-day section hike headed south to Amicalola Falls. I offered to help gather some wood for the fire in exchange for a spot around the campfire. As the sun went down and the moon lit up the sky, we sat and talked about hiking, gear, jobs, and whatever we could think of. They told me of another hiker they ran into earlier that day who was a few miles ahead of me. He was a 77-year-old man that was attempting his fourth thru-hike. They told me I would probably run into him in a day or so. As it got near 9 pm, I excused myself and retreated to my tent. The temperatures were only going to drop to the mid to high 30s but I made sure I placed my water filter in my pocket so it would not freeze and I crawled into my tent. I had survived my first day on the AT and looked forward to some sleep.

The temperatures did not get too cold that night as it stayed above freezing. I woke the next morning as the sun started to peek through my tent. Laying there in my quilt, I was fairly warm but needed to use the bathroom and was dreading crawling out of the warm quilt to do so. I slept ok but did keep waking up through the night, trying to calm my mind down which was in overdrive all night long. I eventually changed out of my sleep clothes and put my hiking clothes back on and emerged from my tent. The section hikers were already up and about and I joined them as I ate some breakfast.

After eating and packing up my gear, I bid farewell to my fellow hikers and finally got moving down the trail at around 10 am. I got turned around a little bit but eventually found the white blaze and started heading north. The sun was shining and the temperature was cool but felt nice as I continued down the trail. As I hiked, I thought about all the people at home and how they were at work and engaged in the daily grind. Even though I was having to be out in the cold and hike mountains, I only had the schedule I created for myself. For the first time in my life, I had complete control over what I was doing and what I did. As I hiked, I was able to actually think about my life and the people I had in my life. There was nobody calling and interrupting me on the phone, nobody asking me to do this or that, nobody doing anything. It was just me and the trail. At times, I could stop walking and just listen to the silence all around me. The bright sun and fresh crisp air acted as a natural mood booster. I realized how lucky I was to be doing what I was doing and did my best to take it all in and appreciate the position I was in.

The trees were, for the most part, bare which while it did not provide much in the way of color, it did provide me with the opportunity to see more of the landscape and more of the views.

As the day went on, I did pass the occasional hiker or local who was out for a walk. I even ran into an elderly gentleman who was walking his dog and was a former thru-hiker. I stopped for a moment to talk and he asked me where I was headed. I responded with, "I'm headed to Maine!" He looked at me with a little shock on his face and responded, "you are early, you are the first one I have seen this year!" I explained I wanted to avoid the crowd and the summer heat and then answered a few more questions before he wished me luck and I pushed northward.

The trail was well maintained but it usually consisted of either climbing up a mountain or climbing down a mountain. As I began to climb each mountain, I would inevitably get pretty winded so I would stop and catch my breath for about 30 seconds and then continue to climb up until I needed another 30-second break (usually not long). As I was climbing one mountain, I could see another hiker that was carrying a huge pack ahead of me. Eventually, as I climbed, I slowly closed the gap between myself and the other hiker. I wound back and forth on the switchbacks that carried me up the mountain and came around a bend in the trail and saw the gentleman I had been following taking a break on a log.

As I approached the man, I stopped and greeted him. "Great day for a hike!" I exclaimed. He responded saying it was a great day but that the mountains can wear you out. I pulled off my pack and grabbed my water bottle to take a drink. As I drank some water and grabbed a snack to eat, I chatted with the gentleman. He introduced himself as Loner Bohner and asked me if I was thru-hiking. I told him I was and introduced myself as Scoutmaster. "Are you a Scoutmaster?" he asked. "Yes, sir! Back in South Carolina," I replied. Loner then proceeded to tell me that he was attempting his fourth thru-hike and asked me to guess his age. "77," I replied. He looked surprised that I knew that but I quickly explained that I had spent the night with a couple of section hikers the night before and they told me all about him.

I commented on the size of his pack and he said it weighed 50 pounds. He told me his plan was to take about 7 months to complete the trail and showed me his AT patch and the three 2,000-miler rocker patches he had sewn on his shirt. As I stood there talking with him, I realized I was speaking to a guy that was definitely a legend on the trail. Once I finished my snack, I hoisted my pack up and secured it to my body. I wished Loner good luck and told him I would probably see him later.

As I continued hiking up the mountain, I could not help but think of Loner. Here was a man that since the age of 60 had completed three thru-hikes and was working on his fourth. On top of that, he was carrying a 50-pound pack compared to my 30 pounds. Meeting him gave me more confidence that I could do this. I knew that, physically, my body would acclimate itself to the daily grind of climbing up and down mountains. My major focus was making sure I listened to my body and while I needed to push myself out of my comfort zone, it was important not to push myself to the point where I risked getting some type of injury that would take me off the trail. I found myself looking at my watch and checking my progress to estimate what time I thought I would be at Woods Hole Shelter, my destination for the day. I started to make up games in my mind to help the time pass as the miles slowly went by. I was averaging about a 2-mile per hour pace and was on schedule to arrive at the shelter around 5 pm which would give me about an hour before night would fall upon me.

I finally approached the blue-blazed spur trail leading to Woods Hole Shelter and hiked the 4/10ths of a mile to the shelter, passing a small stream on the way. When I arrived at the shelter, there was an older gentleman named Copperman already in the shelter and I greeted him before setting up my tent and starting to cook some instant potatoes and tuna for dinner. While I was cooking, Loner came walking into camp and set up in the shelter. The sun was just setting and while I was able to watch the beautiful sunset, the wind was gusting, making me shiver as I still had the damp sweat-soaked clothes on that I hiked in all day. I quickly cleaned up my dinner dishes, brushed my teeth, and placed my food bag in the bear box that was located near the site before retreating from the wind in my tent for the night. In my tent, I was able to change into dry clothes and plan out my next day.

I was camping at the base of Blood Mountain and had to climb about 800 feet in 1.2 miles right out the gate in the morning. Blood Mountain is the highest point of the AT in Georgia and sits at an elevation of about 4,400 feet. The weather was expected to be cloudy and cold with rain coming in the next evening. After climbing Blood Mountain, I would have to descend 1,400' over 3 miles to reach Neel Gap.

My plan was to get to Neel Gap and make a decision then on whether I would stop there for the night or push on. I was lucky enough to have cell service where I could text and check Facebook. I updated my Facebook and was able to check some comments. I was 27 1/2 miles in and felt really good physically. Reading the words of encouragement from friends and family helped to keep my spirits high and motivate me to get to Neel Gap the next day.

The wind blew all night long and would push against the side of my tent but I stayed warm inside my quilt. I slept a little better and started to change back into my hiking clothes as the night faded away and light appeared in my tent. After eating breakfast and packing up most of my gear, I headed to the privy that was located about 75 yards away from the shelter. The privy was not fancy but it was nice to sit down to use the bathroom and have some protection from the wind. There is nothing like taking a poop after two days of hiking. I felt like I must have dropped a couple of pounds and it made me lighter on my feet.

I took my time leaving camp and by the time I rolled out at 9 am, Copperman and Loner had already headed out. I stopped and filtered a couple of liters of water on the way back to the trail and then started my ascent of Blood Mountain. The trail was a series of switchbacks and I climbed through the cold misty air. I would stop every few minutes to catch my breath but would not stay stopped for long as the sweat from the climbing would immediately turn frigid when I was stationary and the wind had a chance to hit me. Every few minutes, I would look at the Guthooks app on my phone to see how much further I had to go. As I hiked, I would try to look ahead on the trail to see if I could see Loner as I knew he only had about a 20-minute head start on me.

Eventually, I spotted him and it took no time for me to close the gap and catch up to him. When I did, we both stopped for a short break and chatted some more. Finally, he motioned for me to go first so he would not slow me down and I accepted. As I got near the top, the wind picked up, the temperature dropped, and the summit became engulfed in a cloud of mist.

Breaking out of the wood line and into the mist-filled summit, I came to Blood Mountain Shelter, the oldest shelter on the AT. It is a stone shelter and with the weather conditions that day, it seemed as if I was in the middle of a horror movie as the shelter looked desolate and unwelcoming. I entered the shelter and while it somewhat protected me from the wind, it felt like I was standing in a freezer as the stone walls provided no insulation from the temperature outside and only seemed to magnify the chilly air. I found the logbook for the shelter and recorded my presence. About that time, Loner arrived and we explored together for a few minutes before heading north and starting our descent into Neel Gap.

The start of the descent was very rocky and I took my time to ensure I did not slip on ice and injure myself. Eventually, the rocks gave way to a decent footpath and I was able to pick up the pace. I passed several day hikers who were making their way up the mountain southbound and greeted them as I hiked on. I was starting to get excited about not only getting to at least stop in at the outfitter's store at Neel Gap and warm up, but also to reach a milestone on the trail.

Neel Gap is at mile marker 31.5 and is a popular point along the trail for northbound hikers to quit their trek. There is a tree outside the shop that contains the boots and shoes of hikers who have ended their journey, deciding a thru-hike is not for them. It is also a popular location for hikers to do a shakedown of their pack and get rid of items they now realize they do not need to bring with them. The outfitter, Mountain Crossings, will do a shakedown for you and you can ship stuff home from their location. Fortunately, all the hiking and camping I did as a Scoutmaster with my troop allowed me to really dial in my gear. While I was doing my research on my hike, I remember seeing hikers get to Neel Gap and here I was almost at the first milestone of the trip.

When I neared the end of my descent of Blood Mountain, I could hear the occasional car driving on the road below me and I knew I was getting close. As I emerged out of the woods, I looked across the road and there was Mountain Crossings. I scurried across the road and as I approached the entrance, I could hear the sound of wind chimes as a slight steady breeze rustled through the trees. I looked up and saw what seemed to be several dozen boots hanging from the branches of one of the trees and felt a sense of accomplishment having made it this far and still feeling motivated to continue. I removed my pack and placed it on the ground along with my hiking poles. Checking my phone, I noticed I had service so I placed a call to Laine. I heard the familiar voice of my wife say, "Hi honey!" and I began to update her on my progress. As we talked, the combination of my damp clothes and the cold air began to make me shiver. I told my wife I was going to check out the store and I would call her back in a little bit. I hung up the phone and made my way into the store.

When I got inside, I saw Copperman already checking out some of the supplies and I decided to get myself something to eat since it was nearly lunchtime. I asked the clerk what they had to eat and he directed me to a freezer of items you could purchase and they would cook for you. I spotted a Red Baron pizza and I grabbed it along with a soda. Before I could get to the counter, Loner came into the shop having made it off the mountain. The clerk rang up my food and told me it would take 15 minutes to cook the pizza. He also asked me if I wanted to get a bunk in the bunkhouse for the night. For $20, I would get a bed and shower. Looking at the weather forecast, the rain was supposed to start around 5 pm and continue into the early evening before stopping. Temperatures were going to drop into the mid-20s overnight and be cold in the morning. It didn't take me long to say yes, especially after hearing Copperman and Loner were both going to stay. I had hit my goal of making it to Neel Gap in three days so I decided to treat myself and take it easy.

When my pizza was ready, I went to the bunkhouse and dumped my pack on a bunk then made myself at home in the kitchen area to eat my pizza. A frozen pizza never tasted so good. After eating, I took a nice hot shower and washed my clothes in the sink and hung them by my bunk to allow them to dry. I sorted my gear in my pack and went back into the store and bought a few food resupply items. Looking at Guthooks, I was only 38 miles from Hiawassee, Ga and my next planned stop. It was Thursday and I wanted to be in Hiawassee by Sunday. After checking out my hike plan, I retreated to my bunk and took a nap.

Around 5 pm, the rain started to come down and a female hiker named Euro came into the bunkhouse having rushed down Blood Mountain in an effort to beat the rain. I had seen her at Amicalola Falls when I was heading out on Day 1. She had hiked the Approach Trail and pulled a big day to get to Neel Gap before the rain. It was February 1st and there were four north-bound hikers in the bunkhouse. Any concern that I was going to be hiking the trail all alone by leaving as early as I did started to fade away.

I slept ok in the bunkhouse but the realization that it would be cold in the morning still occupied my thoughts as I tried to rest up. Checkout time was by 9 am and I was up well before then to eat some breakfast before packing up my gear. Loner decided to take a zero which meant he was going to stay and not hike any miles that day, so I figured that would be the last time I saw him. Copperman and Euro headed out before me and when I headed out, the air was cold and crisp due to the rain and freezing temperatures the night before. The trees and all the branches on them were covered in ice. The forest shimmered in the early morning sun and while it was cold, it was also beau-tiful. Leaving Neel Gap, the trail climbed 800 feet in one and a half miles. As I would learn throughout my journey, towns and trail stops were usually located in a gap which meant that you typically had to descend a mountain to get to town. The flip side of that was when you left town the next day, you usually had a big climb out of town. Add to that a pack that is full of supplies from town and you start to dread leaving.

As I hiked up one side of a mountain and down the other, I was able to stay warm as long as I was moving. Occasionally, I would encounter a hiker out for a short hike or the occasional person taking their dog for a jaunt in the woods. I eventually caught up to and passed both Copperman and Euro and checked my progress along the way. My plan was to stop at the Low Gap shelter which would put me at about an 11-mile day. At the pace I was hiking, I should be there by 3:30 pm which was earlier than I really wanted to stop but the next shelter did not have a water source. Low Gap not only had water, it also had a privy. Since the temperatures were set to drop into the teens overnight, I figured I could get to camp early and build a fire to warm up a bit before going to bed.

The campsite was located right off the right side of the AT and there were several good tenting spots. A little further down from the tenting area was the shelter, a stream, and the privy. I could see that someone was already at the shelter as I approached. Two guys who looked to be in their 20s were at the site and they had a dog with them. I introduced myself and found out that they were buddies and planned on hiking together to Harper's Ferry where the one guy lived and would get off the trail there as the older guy would continue onto Maine with his dog. I filtered two liters of water and headed back to the tenting area to set up my tent and start a fire.

I got my tent set up just in time to see Copperman coming down the trail and heading towards me. I told him about the others in the shelter and he decided to set up his hammock and let the others have the shelter to themselves. I began to collect some firewood as my food was cooking and, a little while later, Euro came walking into the campsite and decided to stay also. I ate dinner and did my best to get a fire started. The wood was pretty damp from the rain the evening before but I did get it started. As the others went about setting up camp and cooking their food, I stood by carefully tending to the fire. I was starting to adjust to trail life and the routine of hiking all day. As compared to a scout camping trip where you hike and camp, a thruhiker hikes, eats and sleeps. I did not want to build too big of a fire because I did not want to have to stay up late waiting on it to die out. I made sure that after enjoying the warmth for a while, I allowed the fire to start dying down as I cleaned out my dinner pot and brushed my teeth in an effort to start winding down.

By the time the sun began to set, I was starting to settle into my tent and began planning my hike for the next day. I had a good 15-mile day ahead of me and a big climb up Trey Mountain to end the day. I texted Laine and updated her on my status and crawled into my quilt. The best part of the day was getting to lay down and roll out my leg muscles with the leg roller I was carrying and then getting into my quilt. With each day that went by, I could feel myself getting more and more acclimated to sleeping on the trail.

I woke up around 4 am and had to pee. I laid there debating whether or not I wanted to get out of my quilt where I was fairly warm and brave the cold temperatures to use the bathroom or wait until daylight. Since it wouldn't be light out until almost 7 am, I decided if I wanted to get any more sleep, I better bite the bullet and answer nature's call. While it was cold getting out of the tent and using the bathroom, nothing felt better than having an empty bladder and crawling back into my quilt. It wasn't long before I started to doze back to sleep.

The sun peeked through my tent and I could hear Copperman moving about outside. I slowly changed into my hiking clothes and emerged from my tent. I walked to the privy and stretched out my tight calves. After eating some breakfast, I packed everything up and checked with the others on their hiking plans for the day. Euro would probably see me at the shelter on Tray Mountain, while Copperman was planning to take his time as he was ahead of schedule to meet up with his wife later in the week. According to Copperman, he checked the temperature during the night when he got up to use the bathroom and it was 12 degrees. All in all, my sleep system performed well and even though I was somewhat chilly overnight, I was still able to sleep pretty decently.

I shouldered my pack and began pushing north as the trail climbed 500 feet over 2 miles. The climb was very moderate but was just enough to get my body to produce heat to keep me warm. The next 6 miles were either flat or slightly uphill which provided for a fairly decent hike. I pulled out my iPod for the first time and allowed myself to be absorbed in music as I navigated the trail and followed the white blazes. Eventually, the trail took me by a shelter where I stopped and took my pack off and ate some lunch. The trail descended 1,000' to Unicoi Gap and then I faced a climb to the summit of Rocky Mountain. After descending down that mountain, I was faced with my last climb of the day, Trey Mountain.

As my legs pushed my body up the mountain, I strained to catch my breath. The mountains in Georgia do a good job of introducing a person to the AT. While the trail is fairly mani-cured and switchbacks aid the hiker in managing the elevation change as you climb, the trail lets you know that you are still just a beginner. One does not conquer the trail. The trail has a way of humbling those that seek to conquer it. As I climbed, I took frequent 30-second breaks to catch my breath. I would breathe as deeply as I could and then put my head down and drive my feet forward. Step by step, I made my way up the mountain. I would look ahead to a white blaze on a tree 50 or so feet ahead and stare down that blaze as my legs pushed my body closer to it. When I reached it, I would pick out the next one and repeat the process. I had one more night out in the cold before I could head into town tomorrow and enjoy a hot shower and a good meal. I kept that thought in my mind and pushed forward.

As I got closer to the summit, the trees started to thin out and more light shone through the branches. Finally, I arrived at the summit and approached a rock outcropping that allowed me to see the spectacular view of the mountains below. As I caught my breath and drank some water, I checked my phone for service. I was only a 1/2 mile from the side trail for the shelter and it was downhill. My phone showed two bars and I dialed my wife. The phone rang on the other end and soon my wife's voice came through. I relayed to her where I was and tried to describe the view I was experiencing. Standing on top of that mountain, I was looking down on a sea of mountaintops that stretched all the way to the horizon. I felt so small and insignifi-cant compared to the vast wilderness that was in the view before me. While my friends and family were back home enjoying a normal Saturday evening, I was here. I was seeing something they could only imagine.

I finished my phone call and descended towards the shelter. Upon arrival, I ran into Zack and Tank who were in the shelter. Zack was the guy with the dog from the previous night. I asked him where his buddy was and learned he had strained something and was staying behind until better. I set up my tent and filtered some water. Euro eventually showed up and decided to stay in the shelter. The weather report was calling for cold temperatures and sleet starting at about 1 am. Since I wanted to avoid the wind that was blowing pretty good and I would be heading into town the next day and would be able to dry out my tent, I decided to stay in my tent.

It was so windy and cold that I cooked and ate in the vestibule of my tent. While the wind was gusty and strong, the tent shielded me from its effects. Although I had to deal with colder temperatures and high winds being near the top of the mountain, it also provided me with cell service where I was able to check and comment on social media. Reading the positive messages from friends and family did wonders for my morale. I was 11 miles from Dick's Creek Gap and Laine had already arranged for a shuttle to pick me up there and take me into Hiawassee for a town stop, warm bed, and hot food.

Around 2 am, I was awakened to the sound of sleet hitting my tent. I hit at the top of my tent and felt a sheet of ice slide off and fall to the ground. Even though the weather was nasty outside, I was dry inside my tent. I rolled over and went back to sleep. When morning arrived, it was still sleeting outside. I grabbed my food bag and ate some breakfast before trying to pack up all the gear I could while remaining in my tent. When I finished, I put on my rain pants and rain jacket and crawled out of my tent. I quickly grabbed my pack and hurried to the shelter and placed it in the shelter where the others were already up and eating breakfast. I then ran back to my tent and quickly pulled out all the stakes and grabbed the entire structure and carried it over to the shelter which had an overhang. While under the protection of the overhang, I was able to break the tent down and shake it off. I packed my tent up and prepared to endure the sleet as I had an 11-mile day ahead of me. When I looked at the forecast, it was scheduled to stop sleeting around lunchtime and then remain cold and cloudy. Zack and Tank were also planning on stopping in Hiawassee, so we headed out together.

Not long after I started hiking, I was trying to be careful as I descended Trey Mountain. With all the sleet and cold temperatures, there were patches of ice on the trail. As I carefully navigated down the trail, I stepped forward with my right foot and hit a patch of ice and did a full spit as I landed on my butt. My Frogg Toggs rain pants split in the crotch but, fortunately, there were no injuries. I picked myself up and continued my descent. The trail continued north and formed a series of PUDs (Pointless Ups and Downs). As I would come to learn, when hiking the AT, you are either climbing up or climbing down. I pushed on through the sleet which made it difficult to snack and drink water but I did my best to keep myself hydrated and nourished to keep up my energy. The sleet began to lighten up as I hiked and by lunchtime it had stopped completely. I got to Addis Gap and then began my biggest climb of the day up to Kelly Knob. The climb was a steep one as I gained 1,000 feet in only one mile. My energy reserves were low and I had to stop every couple of minutes to catch my breath. I thought to myself that if there was a time for me to have a heart attack, now would be a good time. I kept my focus on the hot shower I would be getting in a few hours and the food I was going to be able to eat. I had read about an all-you-can-eat buffet in Hiawassee and I was really looking forward to it. It was also Super Bowl Sunday so I envisioned eating a lot and watching some football.

I finally made it to the top of Kelly Knob and checked Guthooks to see what the terrain looked like from there. There were a few small climbs but most of the remaining miles were downhill and I was excited about that. I was able to reach Dick's Creek Gap and the parking lot before 3 pm and messaged my wife who coordinated with a shuttle driver to pick me up and take me into town. While waiting for my ride, I ate a snack and tried to stay warm. Within a few minutes, a van pulled up with an older lady driving. She got out and greeted me as I put my pack and poles in the van and hopped in the front seat. It was a short ride into town but not short enough to walk. My plan was to get a room at the Budget Inn and within a few minutes, we arrived. I scheduled a pickup for the next morning and then walked into the office and paid $40 for a room with a king-sized bed. After getting my key, I made my way to my room and before I could get there, I saw Zack coming from the room next to mine. He had arrived 30 minutes earlier and was already making himself at home. We chatted and agreed to meet for dinner in a couple of hours after we both had time to shower and I had time to wash some clothes.

I unlocked the door to my room and plopped my pack on the floor. It felt great to be indoors and have a room all to myself. While I enjoyed staying at the bunkhouse at Neel Gap, it was nice to have my own place with my own bathroom. I checked out the accommodations then decided to get some laundry washed so I would have clean and dry clothes to wear for dinner that evening. After checking with the manager to see where the laundry was located, I walked up the road to the drugstore that was nearby to purchase some laundry detergent. While in the store, I bought a large Gatorade, some Hot Pockets, and some other snacks. I hurried back to the room and gathered my laundry. In order to wash all my clothes, I planned on wearing my rain pants and rain jacket as the laundry was in a building across the parking lot from my room. Fortunately, I had some duct tape and was able to tape the crotch of my rain pants together so that I wouldn't flash anyone walking across the parking lot.

As I walked to the laundry room, I realized that I was officially "hiker trash", as I was wearing nothing but some duct taped Frogg Toggs rain pants and a rain jacket with wet muddy shoes. After starting my laundry to wash, I returned to my room and prepared to take a nice hot shower. I thought about this moment all day as I hiked in the cold sleet and climbed several mountains to get here. Once I turned on the shower and stepped under the strong hot stream, I let the water run on my head and could feel my body rejuvenating itself. Simple things like a hot shower are the things you miss the most when you are on the trail. Just a few hours before, I was climbing a mountain in the rain, hungry with no energy in my body and now I was in a hot shower with a Gatorade and some Hot Pockets waiting for me when I got out. Life was good. The trail can throw immense hardships at you one moment, then just a short while later, bring you simple pleasures that seem like miracles.

After showering, eating a snack, and getting my clothes washed, I hung up my tent in the shower and allowed it to dry. Putting on clean clothes still warm from the dryer was pure bliss and I looked forward to getting some dinner. When I was ready, I walked to Zack's room and knocked on his door. He invited me in as he put his shoes and coat on. Tank greeted me and I petted him while I waited on Zack. When he was ready, we walked to Daniel's Steakhouse, known for the all-you-can-eat buffet. The air was cool but it felt good to stretch my legs without shouldering a 30-pound pack. At the restaurant, I gorged myself on fried chicken, fried okra, dressing, turkey, gravy, green beans, and hush puppies. In an effort to feel like I was trying to be healthy, I also hit up the salad bar and piled my plate with lettuce and all sorts of extras. I easily ate three big plates of food and washed it all down with several glasses of sweet tea.

As we made our way back to the hotel, we stopped in at

the grocery store to resupply our food bags. Fortunately, I had already eaten, otherwise, I would have bought too much food if I hadn't stuffed myself full. We gathered our bags and when we arrived, we said goodnight and retreated to our rooms. I dumped my bounty of resupply on my bed and turned on the Super Bowl while I sorted and repackaged my food. When done, I relaxed, called home, and eventually ate my other Hot Pocket and other snacks. As it got later in the evening, I didn't want my town stay to end but at least the weather was supposed to be dry and sunny the next day.

I was only 8 miles away from the North Carolina border. This time tomorrow, I would be camping in North Carolina and I would have completed the first of my 14 states that I needed to hike. I tried to focus on small milestones. Maine and the end of the trail were still so very far away. I constantly told myself to focus on the milestones right in front of me and not focus on the ultimate goal. My plan was to hike around 11 miles tomorrow and that would put me past mile marker 80 and would be the longest hike I had ever done. My next town stop was scheduled to be Franklin, NC which was only 40 miles from Hiawassee. I tried to focus on where the next town stop was going to be and thought of my thru-hike as a series of shorter section hikes. It was the only way to stay focused and not get overwhelmed with the vast number of miles and mountains that existed between Georgia and Maine.

After a fairly restful night's sleep, I got up and took a shower before getting dressed and packing my backpack up. I then walked over to a Subway that was located on the other side of the hotel and got there just as they were opening up for breakfast. I ordered myself a breakfast sandwich on flatbread and also got a foot-long sub sandwich to pack out for lunch and dinner. I met my ride back at the hotel and within minutes I was back at the trailhead and ready to start hiking north again. As usual, I had a climb out of the gap and the climbs seemed to last all day. I would hike up a peak then back down only to be greeted by another peak to climb and descend. I counted at least eight significant climbs during the course of my 11.8-mile hike. I was able to keep my spirits up as I climbed most of the morning because I kept thinking about the Subway sandwich I was carrying in my pack. I was looking forward to being able to stop and take a lunch break and dig into that sandwich.

Finally, around noon, I came across a large log that provided a great place to have a seat and enjoy some lunch. The weather was really nice as the sun was shining and the temperature outside was in the mid-forties. While I was sitting there enjoying my sandwich, I heard someone approaching from behind. Eventually, I saw the image of a man who looked to be in his early sixties, average height and a snow-white beard. When the man reached my position, I greeted him and we exchanged pleasantries. His name was Santa and he was also a northbound thru-hiker. He continued on while I went back to work on my sandwich. When I finished, I took a nice big drink of water and put my pack back on and hit the trail.

I would eventually catch up to Santa and we hiked together for a while and chatted. He was recently retired and was from Georgia. He planned on taking his time but had a wife at home and two grown children. As we talked, we continued to hike and the miles did not seem as tough. I shared my story with him and before I pushed ahead when Santa decided to take a snack break, we probably knew more about each other than some people find out about people after knowing them for months. The trail does that. No one is a stranger on the trail. From the moment you step on the trail, you meet people who are unlike anyone you meet in the outside world. It doesn't take long for hikers on the trail to get to know each other and develop a bond. I knew I would see him again.

About 8 miles in for the day, I came across a wooden sign that was nailed to a tree. Carved into the sign was "NC/GA" signifying the state line separating Georgia and North Carolina. I paused at the sign and snapped a picture of myself standing in front of it. One state down and thirteen more to go.

While Georgia is not one of the longer states, it was definitely a tough one. The trail was fairly manicured and well taken care of, but there were plenty of mountains and climbs that a hiker needed to do. Statistically, there are a lot of hikers who quit in Georgia. Making it through this first state was definitely a milestone and something I could be proud of completing. With each milestone that I reached, my confidence increased. This last day in Georgia was a tough one but I was feeling pretty good about my energy stores. The food and hydration I was able to get in town the day before was definitely a morale booster and what my body needed. By the time I reached the state line, I was happy to wish a fond farewell to Georgia and was happy to see North Carolina... or so I thought.

CHAPTER 3

North Carolina

North Carolina does a wonderful job of punching you in the gut and wishing you were back in Georgia. Even though I was only about three miles from the shelter I planned to stay at that night, my day was going to get harder. When I reached the North Carolina border, the state greeted me with two steep climbs back to back. As I climbed up the peaks, I regretted complaining to myself about Georgia. My only hope was that this start to North Carolina was not a preview of what the state had in store for me.

As I reached the summit of the last climb for the day, I was only 2/10ths of a mile from Muskrat Creek Shelter where I planned to stay. I stopped at the summit and took in the beautiful view that was before me. Excited to be done climbing for the day and excited to be in a new state, I took out my cell phone and luckily had a cell signal. I called Laine and shared with her the events of the day. I wasn't sure if I would have service at the shelter so I chatted for several minutes before pushing forward and arriving at my camp spot for the evening.

I scoped out the site and selected a spot to set up my tent. After getting my tent set up and preparing to cook dinner, Santa came hiking into the campsite. I chatted with him as he set up his hammock and we checked the weather report for the evening. The temperature was going to dip into the high 20s but only a 20% chance of light showers. After dinner, I got in my tent and settled for the night. With each night I spent on the trail, my body started to get used to sleeping outside and I seemed to get better sleep each and every night. The trail was growing on me.

During the night, I woke up to the sound of light rain hitting my tent. I rolled over and went back to sleep, hoping the rain would stop before it was time for me to get up. When the morning light started to creep into my tent, I opened my eyes and listened for the sound of rain on my tent. All I could hear were the birds. The rain had stopped.

It was a Tuesday morning and Day 8 on the Appalachian Trail. As the days came and went, I started to lose track of what day of the week it was as every day was the same. Since it was a weekday, I figured the trail would be pretty empty today. Last weekend I noticed an increase of hikers, both day hikers and weekend and section hikers, as I traveled on the trail. The weekdays provided more solitude. Hiking by myself did not seem to bother me. This trek was the first time I was getting to hike on my own. All my previous hikes were with my scouts. When you are hiking with a bunch of boys ranging in age from 11 to 17, with a few other Dads sprinkled in, you don't really get to hike at your pace. As Scoutmaster, I was responsible for all the others, thus my pace would be dictated by the group and what was going on at the moment.

Hiking the trail alone allowed me to set my own schedule and go at my own pace. When I felt like hiking fast, I would hike fast. If I was tired or wanted to slow down, I could do that too. Having spent nearly 50 years living in "civilization", I realized how programmed I had become to following other people's schedules. Out here on the trail, time took on a new meaning. The worries of the real world started to fade away. I started to forget about my work life and began to accept my new job and purpose. Life was really pretty simple now. Wake up, pack up, and walk. In between that, I would eat a little, drink a little, and do basic hygiene tasks. When the day was over, I would lay down exhausted but satisfied and then repeat the entire thing the next day.

The rain of the night before and the cold temperatures and high elevation caused ice to form in patches along the trail. Add to that the fact I was descending, and I decided to stop and put my micro-spikes on my shoes. I wasn't the most graceful hiker and I knew that one wrong fall could mean the end of my hike and the end of everything I had worked for over the past 7 months. I carefully navigated my way through the ice fields using my hiking poles to help me balance as the trail also contained slick rocks scattered throughout my path. The morning fog and mist had not burned off from the night before but as I descended and the hours passed, the sun came out.

I stopped on a ridge along the trail to take a lunch break and sat down on a rock. I opened my pack and pulled out my food bag. One advantage to the cold weather was that I was able to pack out some food that normally might not last several days on the trail. I pulled out a bagel I had and made a sandwich from that, along with ham and cheese. It tasted so good and was such a treat to eat a sandwich and not have to eat a protein bar or some other bland food. I savored every bite and, for a few minutes, all was right with the world. It was amazing how a simple ham and cheese bagel could make me so happy.

After eating, I packed up my trash and re-shouldered my pack. I had a big climb up and over Standing Indian Mountain but after that, it was mostly downhill except for a short climb before I got to Carter Gap shelter, my goal for the day. Standing Indian was a nearly 1,200-foot climb but it was stretched out over 2 miles. The climb did not seem too bad and definitely looked worse on the map than it was in real life. I don't know if that was reality or if I was starting to get used to climbing mountains. Either way, I was grateful for my performance and my energy levels were pretty good. My feet and legs felt great and I was excited to be making progress.

The sky was cloudy and I did experience a little rain as I hiked but just enough to make me put my rain cover on my pack and my raincoat on my upper half. Eventually, I came to the shelter which was right off the trail and I checked out my digs for the night. We were supposed to get a good bit of rain overnight that was going to continue into the morning. I wasn't really looking forward to having to pack up my tent in the rain and since I would have to stay in shelters in the Smokies, I figured tonight would be a good time to try out the shelter and see how I liked it.

There was no one else at the shelter when I got there and I laid out my sleeping pad and quilt on the left side. The shelter had a covered porch area in the front which was nice as it provided a place to cook in front of the shelter but still have a roof over your head. I had hiked about 12 1/2 miles for the day and was looking forward to a hot meal and some coffee. As I began to get ready to cook, Santa appeared from the trail and joined me at the campsite.

We both discussed the weather report for the next 24 hours and Santa decided to stay in his hammock instead of battling mice with me in the shelter. Both of us were planning on stopping in Franklin, NC which was about 16 miles north. With the rain that was predicted for the evening and morning hours, we both planned on splitting the mileage over two days and getting into Franklin early afternoon on the second day.

After eating my ramen and tuna, I pulled a Starbucks instant latte out of my food bag. I had found these back home and brought a few on my trek. I heated some water and mixed in the instant latte mix. I wasn't worried about the caffeine keeping me from going to sleep but knew that I would probably have to get up in the middle of the night to pee. I sat in the shelter to drink my latte as I watched the sun lower itself behind the trees and nighttime began to fall on the woods around me.

After brushing my teeth and securing my food bag, I made sure my pack was hanging from the hang lines in the shelter and settled in for the evening. Before I could fall asleep, I could hear the footsteps of two mice as they scurried first on the ground in front of the shelter and then up and down the walls and rafters of the shelter. For such a small creature, they sounded like a herd of elephants as they ran around.

As silence returned to the shelter, I started to doze off before being awoken by the stampeding of the small creatures in the rafters above me. Eventually, I pulled the sleeping bag liner over my head and pulled out the iPod and earbuds I brought with me. As I drowned out the noise of the stampeding mice with music from my iPod, I slowly drifted back off to sleep. Except for the occasional need to roll to my side or back onto my back, I slept pretty well. At one point, while sleeping on my back, I felt something run across my forehead and I immediately sat up. Turning on my headlamp, I frantically scanned the shelter looking for the offender. After finding nothing in sight, I laid back down and attempted to go back to sleep, wondering whether I had imagined the entire thing or not.

At some point in the middle of the night, I began to hear the rain as it started to beat down on the roof of the shelter above me. While part of me dreaded having to deal with the rain in the morning, the rest of me was happy to be warm and dry in my quilt. My thoughts went to Santa in his hammock and I wondered if he regretted his decision not to stay in the shelter.

As daylight started to filter in, Santa came into the shelter. He began to make his breakfast and I slowly stretched and began to wake up. The rain was still coming down pretty hard and I had no desire to get out of my warm bag and start hiking in the rain. I tried to check the weather but did not have service on my phone. Fortunately, Santa had service and was able to check the forecast and the satellite images. From the reports he was receiving, it looked like the rain was going to be steady and hard until 10:30-11:00 am. Then it would slack off and stop.

After looking at Guthooks, I decided to wait out the rain and hike nearly 9 miles to a shelter, thus leaving me a little over 7 miles the next day to get to Winding Stair Gap and meet a shuttle to go into Franklin. I took my time packing everything up and had a nice leisurely breakfast. I texted Laine through my Garmin and let her know the plan.

As predicted, the rain started to lighten and by 10:45 am, it was just a drizzle. Santa and I threw on our packs and headed north. Eventually, it stopped raining but several times throughout the day a light drizzle would reappear and let me know that any hope of a sunny day to dry out was not going to happen. As I hiked, the trail at times looked more like a stream than a hiking trail.

I finally arrived at the base of Albert Mountain and saw there was a blue-blazed trail that was a road that went up the mountain and re-joined the AT near the top. Even though it was cold and misty rain was falling, I was not about to get off the AT and follow a blue-blaze trail to avoid what I had been told was a tough climb. I followed the white blazes and, eventually, the trail turned into a rock scramble as I ascended the short but steep mountain. At times, I held both hiking poles in one hand as I used my hands for balance climbing the rocks as I ascended. When I neared the top, the rain started to fall a little more consistently.

I reached the fog-laden summit and came to the fire tower. Visibility was about 20 feet, so I declined to climb the fire tower for the non-existent view and started to descend the mountain. As I descended, the rain and wind were cutting through my clothing and my body. Finally, the trail began to flatten out and I entered a part of the trail that was a fog-laden tunnel. As I hiked on, I realized I was approaching the 100-mile mark on the trail. A sense of accomplishment began to come over me as this was the furthest distance I had ever hiked. Coupled with the fact that I did not have much more to hike for the day and tomorrow was going to be a half day into town, I was feeling pretty good. It was also the longest backpack trip I had taken in terms of days. Each day that went by, I became more and more accustomed to being on the trail.

I stopped to filter some water just before reaching Long Branch Shelter where I planned to stay for the night. Upon reaching the shelter, I checked it out and noticed that it was fairly new, having just been built a few years earlier and it was a double-decker shelter. I was all by myself but expected Santa to be arriving shortly. I got my spot set up in the shelter and while doing so, Santa arrived and started to set up his hammock. Once again, we had the campsite all to ourselves and I had the shelter all to myself.

The weather for the next day was supposed to be sunny and I was excited to make it to another town and resupply. We both ate our dinners and cleaned up our gear before retiring to our separate quarters for the night. I slept well that night but again had to deal with the small scurrying feet of the mice that inhabited the shelter.

After eating breakfast with Santa, we packed up our gear and both headed off together. Santa had a 3-mile hike to meet up with his ride that was going to take him to Gooder Grove Hostel where he planned to spend a few days. I would continue north for another 4 or 5 miles and get to the road crossing at Winding Stair Gap where my wife had arranged a shuttle to take me into town and a night at the Budget Inn.

As we hiked the first 3 miles together, we chatted and the time flew by. When we reached the gap where I would leave Santa, we said our goodbyes knowing we would probably not see each other again on the trail. We had only known each other for three days and spent more of that time hiking separately from each other but it was still tough to say goodbye. As I would learn, the friendships you make on the trail might not be long friendships but they definitely are deeper friendships due to the circumstances of the trail. We wished each other good luck and I turned and headed north.

The sun was shining as I made the final climb before having to descend Winding Stair Gap. It was a pretty mild day out and it was perfect for a hike. Knowing that I was about to get into town and be able to grab lunch there really lifted my spirits and allowed me to enjoy the hike. The trail is full of moments when you are in discomfort or in misery but it also gives you moments when you really appreciate being alive and having the opportunity to be out in nature. When I reached the summit, I text Laine to let her know so that she could notify the shuttle driver.

I made my way down to the highway and reached the parking lot. I took off my pack and pulled out my jacket and put it on. Within a few minutes, a vehicle arrived driven by Jim. He got out of the car and greeted me. Opening up the back, he reached in and grabbed a banana and gave it to me. I placed my pack and poles in the back then climbed in the front passenger seat. We chatted as we drove into town and I learned he was an immigrant who came to this country decades ago and lived in Chicago. After retiring, he moved to Franklin to be near the mountains. He called it "God's country" and since his wife passed away, he spent his time shuttling hikers and always making sure they got their potassium by giving them bananas. Eventually, we arrived at the Budget Inn where I paid Jim and arranged for him to pick me up the next morning.

I checked in and went to my room. It was a little after noon so I decided to get some lunch and resupply before washing some clothes and taking a shower. I walked about a mile across town and stopped at a Hardees for lunch. While waiting in line to order, there was an older gentleman who ordered a cheeseburger and wanted Swiss cheese instead of American cheese on his burger and was making a big deal out of it, making sure they would substitute cheeses for him. He finally finished his order and I thought to myself that I was just grateful to be here getting to order a burger and fries and this guy is complaining about what kind of cheese will be on his burger.

They handed the man his order and he took his food and headed to his seat. As I got my order and proceeded to a table, I saw the man checking his burger and getting up to return it. They apparently gave him American cheese instead of Swiss. As he stood at the counter complaining, I smiled to myself and started to eat my food. It felt so good to be enjoying a burger, fries and soda after spending the last several days in the woods hiking in the rain and having to deal with mice running across my head as I tried to sleep.

I sat there by myself and looked around the restaurant as I ate. I observed and listened to all the people who were eating their lunch. I wondered to myself if they realized how fortunate they were to be able to walk into a place and have a meal served to them. It made me appreciate being in town. The sun was shining, I was enjoying some good food, I had the rest of the day and night off, and I had the right kind of cheese on my burger. Life was good.

I finished my food and walked next door to the Dollar General to resupply. As I walked through the store, I was able to find all the things I needed. I know the cashier was probably thinking to herself "what the hell is this guy doing?" as she rang up ramen, tuna, candy bars, and a variety of other "high performance" thru-hiker food. "Are you hiking the trail?" she asked as she placed a box of Nature Valley granola bars in a bag. "I am," I replied and then paid for my stash of food and grabbed my bags before heading back to my motel room.

Back at the motel, I went through what would become a ritual of dumping my resupply onto the bed and separating it all out to make sure I bought what I needed to get me to the next town and resupply. I took everything out of its boxes and threw away whatever packaging I did not need to lighten the load as much as possible. I then loaded it all in my food bag and went about my way showering and doing my laundry.

Even though I was in town, I had no cell service, but fortunately, I had Wi-Fi through the motel and was able to Skype with Laine. Since it was a Thursday, I made arrangements to Skype later on in the evening when Laine and my son were at the scout meeting so I could say hello to the scouts and their parents.

I finished my call and decided to walk to the local outfitter in town, Outdoor 76, and see if I could find a pair of rain pants to replace the Frogg Toggs that had split in the crotch. I walked around the store but did not find what I wanted. It was a pretty cool outfitters and the staff was really nice. They had a banner they were asking all thru-hikers to sign, so I grabbed a marker and signed my trail name on it. Leaving the store, I walked past several other shops and restaurants but decided to just get something to eat that I could take back to my room.

I stopped at a Domino's pizza and got myself a cheesesteak and salad for dinner. While waiting for my food, I began a conversation with the manager and discovered he was from South Carolina. We chatted about places we both knew and, eventually, the topic turned to what brought me to town. When I explained to him that I was hiking the Appalachian Trail, he asked where I started. I told him Georgia and saw the look in his face. "Wow," he stated, then asked me how many miles I had hiked so far. "109," I said proudly, and then he asked the next question that I would hear many times over, "how far are you going?"

"Maine," I said. "I am walking to Maine." He looked at me with a sense of awe and asked me how far it was to Maine. "2,190.9 miles," I stated and waited for his response. "That's amazing," he said. It was a scenario that would play out over and over again whenever I met someone and they asked me what I was doing or how far I was hiking. People who are unfamiliar with hiking and the Appalachian Trail do not know what or where Mt. Katahdin is, so I always answered with "Maine" whenever they asked where I was going.

After eating dinner, I waited for the call from Laine on Skype. About 7:30 pm, my phone rang and it was Laine. It was good to see and hear not only her face and voice but to see all the scouts and parents. Being on Skype, I was able to see everyone and they could see me. While it was hard to be sitting there in the motel room and not be at the scout meeting like I normally would be on a Thursday night, it also gave me the motivation to continue on my journey and make sure I went all the way.

I finished my phone call and prepared to get some sleep so I could be fresh in the morning. I fell asleep with no problem but woke up in the middle of the night sweating. After sleeping out in the cold for most of the last week and a half, I was not used to sleeping in a warm room. I fell back to sleep but still woke early enough to shower, eat, and get all packed up before Jim came to pick me up at 8:00 am.

Jim gave me another banana and, as we drove back to the trail, he told me about how he ended up in Franklin and in America. He was an immigrant and came to this country and built a life for himself. He was a widower with grown children and was retired. He enjoyed shuttling hikers as he got to meet a lot of different people from all over the country and the world. We pulled up to the trailhead and I retrieved my pack and poles. I waved goodbye to Jim and then paid and thanked him for the ride. I turned away and headed back into the woods and back up into the mountains.

I was only 55 miles from Fontana Dam where Laine was scheduled to come and see me for the first time since I left from Springer Mountain. Since it was a Friday and I was planning on meeting Laine on Monday, I had 4 days to cover the miles to get to see her. It was a beautiful sunny day today but the weather forecast was not looking good for Saturday and Sunday as rain was predicted for both days. Having mapped out my plan for the day the night before, I planned on going 15.8 miles to get to a shelter.

The trail started with a 1,400-foot climb before descending and ascending four more times before reaching the Cold Spring Shelter where I planned on staying for the night. Along the way, I fell hard twice but, fortunately, did not injure myself. When I got to the small 6-person shelter, there was someone there trying to keep a fire lit. I could tell by the looks of him that he was not a thru-hiker and wasn't even a section hiker.

As you spend more time on the trail, you start to be able to recognize hikers. You can tell by their clothing, gear, and what they pack out for food whether they are a hiker and what type of hiker. The man was having a difficult time keeping the fire going as all the wood in the area was pretty damp from the rain earlier in the week. He was wearing a big heavy cotton-hooded sweatshirt, had a large fixed blade knife on his belt, and was using a one-gallon milk jug as a water bottle. I said hello and introduced myself. We began to talk and I asked where he was from. He told me he was from Connecticut and had come south to North Carolina with his ex-boss. I found out he was in construction and had decided to take a hike for a few days and was heading south from the Nantahala Outdoor Center (NOC) to Franklin.

He seemed ok as I spoke with him but it was pretty strange for this guy to decide to take a hike in early February with gear that looked like he got at the local surplus store. I figured he might be homeless and was just going from shelter to shelter. After we ate dinner and the sun started to go down, we both started to get ready to go to bed. As I got into my quilt and the sky turned dark, the other hiker pulled an iPad from his bag and started to watch the movie Pulp Fiction. He was definitely a strange guy but I was too tired to care. I closed my eyes and drifted off to sleep.

I woke when the daylight started to invade the shelter and went through my morning ritual of using the privy, packing up, and eating some breakfast. It had rained during the evening but was not raining as I prepared to get on the trail. I said good-bye to my fellow hiker and started heading north. I had a short climb as I left the shelter but had a bunch of downhills on the agenda for the day as I made my way to the Nantahala Outdoor Center (NOC). I hiked in and out of a few sprinkle showers in the morning and made my way to the last summit of the day, where I was able to stop and eat some lunch.

After getting some food in me, I made my way down the 4 1/2-mile descent toward the NOC. It was a steep descent and the first mile or so was very rocky and rough. I could feel the toll the descent was taking on my legs and knees despite trying to alleviate the slamming of my legs on the trail by using my trekking poles to absorb the brunt of the descent. Both legs were hurting and when I got within 3 1/2 miles of the NOC, a steady rain began to fall and a steady wind began to pick up.

According to the weather reports, the rain that was starting was part of a large system that was coming from Texas and it was expected to continue raining for the rest of the day and evening and throughout the next day. Even though I had enough food to get me to Fontana Dam, I had contemplated stopping at the NOC and getting a bunk in an effort to dry out before heading back out in the rain the next day. According to Guthooks, the restaurant was open and they had bunkhouses available for $45 a night. While I really did not want to pay that since I just stayed in town two days ago, the current and upcoming weather made up my mind for me.

As the rain and wind beat down upon me, I focused on the trail in front of me, making sure I did not slip on the slick rocky and muddy trail. I made my way down and could hear the wind cutting through the forest and the trees swaying and creaking as I hiked. At one point, I looked up and squinted through the raindrops as I heard a terrible crash echoing throughout the forest. I could not see the cause of the crash but it was obvious that a tree was uprooted due to the saturated ground and strong winds and crashed to the forest floor. Every creaking tree I passed, I prayed they did not topple over on me. Having my trip, and possibly life, end because I got crushed by a falling tree was not something I wanted. I put my head down and just tried to hike as fast as I could without slipping and falling.

As I hiked, I could hear the voices of a man and woman as they called out a name. It was obvious they were calling for their dog and it wasn't long before I met up with them as they were headed in the opposite direction to me up the mountain. They asked if I had seen a little dog and I replied no. They were hikers out for the day with their dog and he had gotten lost. As

I continued to hike, I looked for the dog but had no luck finding him. Knowing what animals live in the woods and having just heard a pack of coyotes the night before, I felt bad for the dog and its owners.

All of a sudden, 50 feet in front of me, a gust of wind grabbed a hold of a tree on the side of the trail. Before I could do anything, I watched the roots emerge from the ground and saw the tree come crashing to the ground. Fortunately, it fell away from the trail and was 50 feet in front of me but it made me pick up my pace. All I wanted to do was get to the NOC.

I eventually passed a shelter off the right side of the trail and I knew that meant I was only a mile from the NOC. I sped up my pace as the descent softened, and soon, I was emerging from the woods and at the NOC. I walked over to the outfitters to see about getting a bunk for the night but was told since it was off-season I have to go to the restaurant to rent a room. I walked into the restaurant and enjoyed the feeling of not having the rain beating down on me. I was soaked to the bone but did not care. I had made it to the NOC and was minutes away from dry clothes and a hot meal.

I booked a bunk room and headed out of the restaurant, then started to head towards the lodging rooms. As I crossed the footbridge that spanned the river, I saw a few river guides navigating the rapids as the rain continued to fall. At the other end of the footbridge was a parking lot and a man stood there and looked at me as I approached. "Does this dog belong to you?" He asked. "Nope but I know who he does belong to," I replied. I then explained to him about the day hikers and he told me that the dog was just found sitting next to one of the cars in the parking lot in the rain. I explained that I was sure they would be back soon.

After getting to my room and changing into some dry clothes, I made my way back to the restaurant to get some dinner. On the way, I passed the day hikers and got to witness the reunion with their dog. My day was getting better and better. At the restaurant, I ordered the biggest burger they had, fries, a salad, and even dessert. All was good and right with the world. Despite the rain, I was dry, fed, and happy.

After dinner, I went back to my room and made sure I dried out all my gear on the wall unit heater that was in my room. I had phone service and great LTE, so I was able to upload some videos and talk to Laine. I was getting excited to see Laine in less than 48 hours but I still had 27 1/2 miles to cover over the next day and a half and the weather was looking rough. When I checked my weather app, I could see nothing but green and yellow on the satellite imagery for the rest of the night and for most of the next day. Added to that was the fact that I had a huge climb to get out of the NOC the next morning. Looking at my camping options, I was planning on doing a 16.2-mile day tomorrow which would be the longest day of my trip so far. The only thing that kept me motivated was the fact I would see Laine on Monday and have my first zero-day on Tuesday.

I woke before my alarm went off, which was starting to become a habit. I packed up my gear as I listened to the rain beat down outside. By the time I headed out, the rain had subsided a good bit but as I hiked, it would rain on and off all day. The trail was saturated and, in several sections, it was unrecognizable. It resembled a stream in some parts and as I made the 8 1/2-mile climb leading out of the NOC, I resigned myself to the fact that I would be wet all day. While I was stopped taking a break at one point, I heard the sound of hiking poles approaching from the rear and I turned around to discover Euro coming up behind me. I hadn't seen her since the night before Hiawassee and it was good to see a familiar face.

We hiked and chatted for a while as we climbed up the 3,000-foot elevation gain out of NOC. Near the top, Euro stopped to take a break and I continued on. As I was hiking, I received a text from my wife letting me know she was heading out on her way to Greenville, SC to stay with her Mom that night before driving the rest of the way to Fontana Dam in the morning. It was great to hear that she was on her way as it motivated me even though the trail was tough and the weather was poor.

As I hiked in and out of the rain, I just kept focused on the fact that in less than 24 hours, I would be dry, warm and be with Laine. I also knew that in my backpack I had some nice dry clothes and as soon as I made it to the shelter that night, I could get out of the wet clothes I was wearing and put on those dry ones. I drew ever closer to the shelter as the day wore on and eventually came to the blue-blazed trail leading one-third of a mile to Brown Fork Shelter.

I arrived at the shelter and was the only person there. I quickly filtered some water and then peeled off my wet clothes and put on some dry ones. As I started to make some dinner, Euro arrived and joined me in the shelter. It was a long, tough day but my demeanor was improving since I was now dry and warm and enjoying a hot meal of ramen and tuna. It was my biggest day on the AT so far but I survived. Despite the miles and the elevation and despite the rainy weather, I was dry and safe and had a half day of hiking tomorrow before seeing my wife.

I woke up the next morning after sleeping for nearly 12 hours and was ready to hit the trail a little after 8 o'clock. Euro was still packing up and was planning to pick up a resupply package at the Post Office at Fontana Village before they closed at 3:45 pm. I asked her if she was staying at the Lodge or at the shelter and she planned on staying at the shelter so she could hit the Smokies first thing the next morning. I was excited to see Laine and didn't want her waiting on me, so I headed out before Euro and hiked the one-third of a mile on the blue-blazed trail until it intersected the AT. I hung a right and headed north excited to get to Fontana Dam. The sun was starting to peak out of the clouds and the more I hiked, the more the sun came out.

The trail looked pretty decent when I checked out the elevation profile and there was only one real ascent I would have to do before starting the descent into Fontana Dam.

I had 11.3 miles to hike to get to where I was going to meet Laine and I kept checking my pace to make sure I was on time to meet her. As I made the final descent and could see the parking lot by the marina, I saw Laine's car pulling into the parking lot. Once I emerged from the woods, she was just getting out of the car and I hiked over to meet her and give her a big hug. It felt great to see her again and all I could think about was getting to spend the next couple of days with her.

After checking into our room at the Lodge, I was able to take a nice hot shower and change into some clothes that Laine brought me. Since it was about 2 pm, the restaurant was in between lunch and dinner services, so we headed to the Fontana Pit Stop to get some lunch. The Pit Stop was basically a gas station but they did serve hot dogs, nachos, and beer. We sat at the counter and had one of the best lunches I ever had. I don't know if the food was really that good or if I just enjoyed it so much because Laine was with me and I had the day off tomorrow.

I decided to leave my laundry and resupply chores to do on my zero-day and just spend the rest of the day relaxing and spending time with Laine. We had a great meal for dinner at the restaurant in the Lodge and a great night sleep in the room. I had made it through two weeks on the trail and had a day off before hitting the Smokies on Wednesday morning.

The next morning, Laine and I were heading to the restaurant to get some breakfast and I spotted Euro sitting in the lobby. I walked up to her and asked her what was up. I introduced her to Laine and asked her if she made it the day before in time to get her resupply box at the Post Office. She explained to me that after I left the shelter that morning, she got packed up and was a few minutes behind me leaving the shelter. When she got back to the AT from the blue-blaze trail, she turned left and hiked 2 miles back the way she came the day prior before realizing her mistake. She turned around and retraced her steps but her error added 4 miles onto her trek and she wound up getting to Fontana Dam after the Post Office was closed for the day.

Since she needed the resupply before starting the Smokies, she spent the night at the Lodge and was now having to wait until 11:45 am when the Post Office opened to be able to get her package. She then planned on starting the Smokies in the afternoon but her mistake cost her a day. I could tell from her demeanor that she was frustrated for having gone the wrong way and I asked her if she needed a ride to the Post Office but she had already arranged for one. I wished her luck and told her that I would probably see her on the trail.

Laine and I spent my off day doing a few chores and trying not to think about the fact that we would leave each other again the next day. The trail forces you to try to live in the moment and not worry about the next day. At the time, I was with Laine and did not have to be cold, wet, or hiking up mountains. I did my best to savor every minute with her and not think about what the next day would bring.

Wednesday morning came sooner than I wanted but I knew that I needed to push back against my feelings and do what I needed to do to accomplish my goal. It was February 14th, Valentine's Day, and while I was happy to see Laine on Valentine's Day, it was a bit bittersweet that I would have to leave her again. We packed up our stuff and checked out of the hotel. I got into the car and stared out the window as we drove back to the marina. Arriving at the trailhead, we said our goodbyes and hugged and kissed before I headed up into the woods and disappeared from sight.

CHAPTER 4

Welcome to the Smokies

After hiking through the woods for a bit, the trail brought me past the Fontana Hilton, a shelter located before the dam that was touted as one of the nicest shelters on the trail. I crossed the dam and as I did, I looked up to my right and could see the Great Smoky Mountains waiting on me. With over 70 miles of the AT running through the Smokies, I would reach the highest point on the AT, Clingman's Dome, and would spend most of my time above 5,000 feet. The Smokies were well known for their unpredictable weather and snow was a serious possibility. There really weren't any places to resupply and it was the largest black bear habitat in the country. On top of that, I had to climb over 3,000 feet in elevation and the weather was calling for possible rain. The good news was that temperatures were expected to be in the 50s.

As I began the long climb into the Smokies, I took my time and regularly checked my GPS to see the progress I was making. After eating some lunch, I continued to hike and passed two section hikers who were traveling south. I nodded and said hello. Little did I know that I would only see one other human being for the next three days.

The rain held off all day but the temperatures remained in the 50s, which, coupled with all the climbing I did, my clothes were soaked with sweat. As the miles and day passed by, I began to get my mind back on the trail and started to get over the sadness I felt earlier in the day when I had to leave Laine. Her next visit was scheduled to be in Virginia in about 4-6 weeks. All I could do at this point was just focus on hiking north and making miles.

I finally arrived at Mollies Ridge Shelter and immediately went and filtered my water for the night. It wasn't even 5 pm but since you are required to stay in shelters in the Smokies, the next shelter was three miles away and did not have a water source, I decided to call it a day. It turned out to be a good decision as it wasn't long after I finished dinner and got my food bag hung that it started to rain. For the first time on the trail, I had the campsite all to myself. The rain continued all through the night but stopped before I woke up.

I took my time getting on the trail the next morning but was still hiking before 9 am. As the morning went on, the sun burned off the clouds and the sky brightened up. I climbed to the top of Rocky Top and decided to stop and eat lunch. The sun was shining brightly and the temperatures were mild. I sat on a rock and took in the view. Looking out in front of me, all I could see was mountain after mountain. A green sea of beauty and no sound except for the occasional breeze. I thought back to the people at home and for one of the first times, I was able to relax and take a real lunch break and realize how lucky I was to be sitting there. It was a Thursday and most people back at home were at work and caught up in the rat race. While the climb up Rocky Top was tough, the view was well worth the effort. This was my new job and purpose in life, I climb mountains, that's what I do.

After eating lunch, I headed north and reached the top of Thunderhead Mountain before starting a descent down toward Beechnut Gap. Before reaching the gap, I came across a spectacular view to the east and stopped to see if I had any cell service. Showing that I had a couple of bars of service, I was able to call Laine and talk to her for a while. It was nice hearing her voice and being able to have decent weather to hike in. After speaking with her for a few minutes, I hung up and called a former co-worker and friend of mine, Eric. It was good to speak with him and I filled him in on my adventures from the last couple of weeks. It was really cool to be hiking through the Smokies and chatting with a friend from home. Since I had not seen any other humans for over 24 hours, it was at least nice to talk to one.

I continued north and eventually made it to Derrick Knob Shelter, my home for the night. I filtered some water and set up camp in the shelter. No one else was around so I checked to see if I had service and, luckily, I did. I decided to try and give my son, Joe, a call and I was able to get a hold of him. It was good to talk to him and fill him in on my progress. I was 189.4 miles in on the trail and would not only hit the 200-mile mark tomorrow but I would pass the 2,000-mile mark left to go on the trail.

For a second straight night, I not only had the entire campsite all to myself, but it would rain most of the night. Fortunately, the temperatures were not dropping too much at night so it wasn't too bad. When I woke in the morning, it was cloudy and foggy but no rain. The forecast was calling for rain in the afternoon and temperatures to drop to about 40 degrees. Considering it was mid-February in the Smokies, I could not complain.

I headed out and shortly after leaving camp, I came across a bunch of sticks on the ground that were arranged and spelled out the number 2,000. That number was there to let southbounders know that they were 2,000 miles into their journey and let northbounders know they still had 2,000 miles to go. As I looked at the number, I wondered what the southbounders felt when they saw it. I wondered what I would feel when I was in that position. For now, I just took satisfaction in the fact that I had less than 2,000 miles to go.

As I continued to hike, I gained elevation. Starting the day around 4,400 feet, I climbed and descended all morning and eventually started the big climb up to the highest point on the entire Appalachian Trail. Clingman's Dome was listed at over 6,600 feet and I was on pace to get to the summit sometime in the early afternoon. Around noon, as I pushed myself up the mountain, the rain they had been predicting all day began to fall. I was wearing a t-shirt and shorts that were already soaked with sweat from all the climbing that day, so I didn't even bother to put on my rain jacket when it started raining.

I finally reached the summit but opted to continue hiking rather than going off trail to climb the observation tower because the top of the mountain was in complete white-out conditions and there was no view at all. In addition, the rain and wind were starting to pound my body and I could feel a definite drop in the temperature. I was 5 miles away from the shelter I was planning on staying at for the night so I started my descent.

I tried to go at a fast pace to keep my body temperature up as the rain and wind was quickly sapping the heat from my body. I contemplated several times stopping and adding some layers but I kept telling myself that I could get warm when I got to the shelter and took off the wet clothes and put some dry ones on. Hypothermia was a real threat but I was able to generate just enough body heat to keep me safe.

As I descended, I kept my focus on the trail below my feet, making sure my footing was secure so that I did not slip and fall. As I placed my right foot down on some gravel that was lining the trail with a one-inch layer of water on top of it, my foot sank completely up to my ankle in thick mud that was lying beneath the rock. I pulled my foot straight up and felt the suction of the mud as I pulled my foot out, revealing a thick coat of mud covering my entire right foot.

I continued forward and, within a few minutes, my left foot discovered a similar sinkhole and also sunk deep into a mud abyss. At least they are both covered in mud I thought to myself and since both feet were completely soaked, I searched for any standing water I could find to soak my feet in and help wash off the mud.

I was visibly shaking as the rain and dropping temperatures were stealing any body heat I was producing as I hiked. I kept checking my GPS and watch just hoping the miles would fly by and I could get to the shelter as soon as possible. I no sooner got my shoes fairly washed off when I submerged my right foot in another mud puddle. Pushing forward, I continued hiking and eventually made it to the trail intersection for the Mt. Collins Shelter. It was a 1/2 mile blue-blaze trail off the AT to the shelter but I was glad to see it. Most of the trail was covered in water as the shelter was at a lower elevation and all the rain was draining along the trail. I got to the shelter and dropped my pack off before heading another one-tenth of a mile down the spur trail to a spring to collect water.

Once back at the shelter, I stripped off my wet clothes and put on some dry ones. I set up my sleep system in the shelter and got busy cooking my dinner. I quickly scoffed down my dinner and cleaned up and got ready to settle in for the night. I was all alone for a third straight night and had not seen anyone all day. I did pass a hiker who was hiking south yesterday but after three days in the Smokies, I had seen only three other human beings.

That would change tomorrow as I was only 5 miles away from Newfound Gap Road, a common tourist spot with a parking lot and restrooms. My plan was to hike there in the morning and meet up with my cousin who lives in Tennessee. I would be able to resupply, wash clothes, get some good food, and have a decent place to sleep for the night. The weather report for tomorrow was calling for more rain and cold temperatures starting later in the morning and lasting throughout the day. Being able to dry out and resupply would allow me to be ready to finish out the Smokies strong. The weather was due to clear up after tomorrow so I was pretty excited to get some good sleep and get to Newfound Gap as soon as I could.

I woke up early and got moving as the darkness lifted and the light seeped into the shelter. I only had 5 miles to hike so I headed out and, within a few minutes, I was re-joining the AT and heading north again. Most of the trail was downhill with only one moderate climb but I kept a good pace and did my best to navigate the wet trail. When I approached Newfound Gap Road, I could hear the sound of cars passing up and down the road. After three days of relative solitude, it was nice to hear some life and know that a break from the trail was approaching fast.

As I approached the road and the woods began to thin out, I saw what appeared to be a blue cooler just inside the trail. My heart began to race as I was excited to think I might be experiencing my first "trail magic" on the trail. Trail magic is a random act of kindness, usually in the form of food, drinks, a ride into town, or just about anything else that is provided to hikers to help make their trek more enjoyable. Those individuals that perform trail magic are known as "trail angels". They are usually former hikers or individuals that just want to help others out. They are the lifeblood of the AT and every thru-hiker that hikes the trail never forgets receiving trail magic. It usually appears when a hiker needs it the most.

I approached the cooler and saw a sign taped to the top announcing it was trail magic for thru-hikers and to help ourselves. I opened the lid and saw a cooler full of drinks, food, and other supplies that would be helpful to a hiker. Since I was going to be in town in a couple of hours, I decided to just grab a banana and a Pepsi. Fresh fruit was something you don't get on the trail and something you don't include in your resupply, so it was a natural choice to select a banana when I had the chance. I scoffed down the banana and cracked open the Pepsi. I lifted the can to my lips and downed the entire thing in one motion. After drinking nothing but water for days, it was nice to have something with some flavor and some sugar.

I prepared to cross Newfound Gap Road and enter the parking lot while the wind was blowing pretty strong and the rain that was predicted for today was starting to fall. The temperatures were a raw 45 degrees and I was glad to be getting off the trail for the rest of the day. I approached the North Carolina - Tennessee state line sign and saw a family of four taking each other's picture in front of the sign. I walked over and offered to take a family photo of all of them and they accepted. They were visiting the area and were happy to get a group shot in front of the sign.

After taking their picture, they offered to take my picture and I handed them my phone. We talked for a few minutes and they asked where I was hiking. I told them I was hiking to Maine via the Appalachian Trail. The Dad asked me where I started and how long I had been hiking. After telling them, I looked at their little boy and told him, "the best thing is, I only have to take a bath once or twice a week!" The little boy smiled and his Dad asked him if he wanted to do that when he grew up. He just smiled. I thanked them for the picture and they wished me well on my journey.

As I was turning to walk away, I heard a female voice yelling, "Scoutmaster!" from across the road and I looked up to see a female running across the road and parking lot. She was waving her hands at me and appeared to know me. When she got near me, she introduced herself as Tina and told me she had been following my journey on YouTube and was the person responsible for leaving the trail magic at the trailhead. I thanked her for the snacks and told her it was the first bit of trail magic I had received on the trail. While we were chatting, a guy in his late 20s walked up and introduced himself, asking if I was thru-hiking. I told him I was and he stated he had thru-hiked the trail a few years before. All three of us stood there and talked about the trail for several minutes before they wished me luck and went on their way.

I headed toward the restroom to not only use the facilities but to get out of the wind and rain that was picking up. My cousin was on her way but would be a little while so I alternated spending time between the restrooms and the parking lot. Despite the weather, it was a Saturday so there were a decent flow of visitors pulling into the parking lot to use the facilities and to try to catch a glimpse of the view which was rapidly deteriorating as the weather worsened.

While I waited, I thought about the last time I was at this parking lot. I came the weekend before Thanksgiving and did a quick hike up to Charlie's Bunion with my cousin. The weather was cold, dreary, and very windy, much like it was today. I remember thinking that the next time I would be here I would be over 200 miles into my trek. It felt really good to be this far but I still had almost 2,000 more miles to go.

My cousin, Kathy, arrived at the parking lot and we drove back out of the Smokies and hit a grocery store to resupply before heading to her apartment for the rest of the day and evening. After a much-appreciated hot shower and homemade dinner, I relaxed and planned out my next few days of hiking.

In the morning, her son, David, picked me up and treated me to breakfast before taking me back to the trailhead. It was a beautiful sunny day and the temperature was 70 degrees. Since it was such beautiful weather and a Sunday afternoon, the trail was packed with tourists and day hikers as I made my way up to Charlie's Bunion. After getting past the popular viewing point on the trail, the crowds disappeared and I did not see another person until reaching the shelter that evening.

The next morning started out cloudy but the sun broke through before lunchtime and stayed out the rest of the day as I made it to Cosby Knob Shelter at the 231-mile mark. The weather was mild and the view was beautiful as I took in the sights in what would be my last night in the Smokies. I was 10 miles away from escaping the Smokies and, more importantly, escaping them without hitting any severe weather. It was the middle of February and I was going to have my third consecutive day of 60-70 degree temperatures in the Smokies.

After a great night's sleep, I packed up and began the 10-mile mostly downhill trek out of the park. About seven miles into the day, I came across a sign that read "Scoutmaster - Lunch at shelter" and pointed down the short blue-blazed trail to the Davenport Shelter. I took the spur trail and arrived at the shelter to find a husband and wife, trail names Lipstick and Free Tickets, waiting for me with fried chicken, cornbread, and Pepsi. They were subscribers to my YouTube channel and had contacted Laine to arrange bringing me lunch.

Even though I was going to meet my mother-in-law at Interstate 40 in about 3 miles to hit town for the evening, I was not about to pass up some trail magic and a chance to visit with some true trail angels. I spent 45 minutes eating and chatting with total strangers and it was a wonderful and humbling experience. Here were two people who did not know me at all but they took time out of their day to put together a huge meal for me, drive to the trailhead, hike a mile uphill with all the food and drinks and sit in the woods waiting for me to arrive. As I spent more and more time on the trail, my faith in human beings was beginning to be restored. Back home, I knew a lot of people who were friends and acquaintances of mine but they were absorbed in their own lives and absorbed in the "civilized" world. The further I went on this hike, the more I learned about people.

I thanked my angels and shouldered my pack and raced to finish the last three miles of the Smokies and meet my mother-in-law, Judy, and her friend, Ed, for a nice town stop and a hotel for the night. I had spent all or parts of 7 days in the Smokies and the temperature never got below 40 degrees. I reminded myself how lucky I was to have such a nice streak of weather in February in the Smokies. I also knew it was too good to be true and somewhere down the line I was going to pay for that good fortune.

CHAPTER 5

Settling In

After spending the night in a hotel and getting dropped off at the trailhead, I started climbing back into the mountains. It was my 23rd day on the trail and it was mostly uphill but the temperatures were still pretty warm. With all the climbs and the 70-degree temperatures, I was consuming lots of water as I was trying to do my best to stay hydrated. It was nice not to have the cold temperatures but I would sweat a ton when I was climbing those mountains.

Since it was a Wednesday, the trail was pretty empty and I had a lot of alone time as I hiked up and down the mountains. As the afternoon went on, I drew closer and closer to Max Patch, a grassy bald that was one of the most talked about parts of the southern portion of the trail. I got to the summit around 4:30 pm and it did not disappoint. There were a few other day hikers on the summit as there is a parking lot less than a mile from the top. It was a sunny and clear day and I paused at the top to take a break and take in the beautiful scenery.

I was only 2 miles from the shelter I planned on staying at for the night, so I headed down the trail and arrived with plenty of time to get set up and eat dinner before it got dark. As I was cooking, I heard voices coming down the trail and I looked up to see it was two male hikers. As they got closer, I immediately recognized Zack being followed by Zack's buddy that I met on Day 4. They had reunited and were doing well. Zack's dog, Tank, was staying with his Dad while he hiked through the Smokies and he was planning on meeting his Dad in Hot Springs to pick him up. Dogs are not allowed in the Smokies and hikers have to either board them or make arrangements for them as they hike that section of the trail.

I was 17.9 miles from Hot Springs and was originally thinking of going 15 miles to a shelter, spend the night, and then doing a late breakfast in Hot Springs, resupplying, and continuing to hike. I had heard a lot of good things about Hot Springs and after talking to Zack, I was seriously considering busting out the nearly 18 miles tomorrow and staying at a hostel as a reward for hitting another daily mileage record.

The temperatures only got down to the 50s overnight and it rained but was clear by morning. I got packed up before the others and hit the trail as I wanted to make sure I got to town at a decent time so I could shower, eat, and resupply before it got too late. I hit some easy trail first thing and I tried to make good time. I could tell that my stamina was improving and I was starting to find my stride. The trail was starting to grow on me and I was making good progress. I got to Hot Springs and booked a room at Elmer's Sunnybank Hostel for $25. After eating dinner at the Smokey Mountain Diner, I resupplied at the Dollar General and retired back to my room.

In the morning, I headed north on the trail through town and crossed the French Broad River then headed into the woods and up into the mountains. As I was climbing the switchbacks, I thought I saw someone ahead of me. After a few minutes, I was gaining on the person and was able to tell it was a female hiker. When I caught up to her, I said hello and we began to talk. Her trail name was Fun Size and she was a northbound hiker attempting to complete her third long-distance trail in as many years. She had completed the Pacific Crest Trail in 2016, the Continental Divide Trail in 2017, and now was on her way to completing the Appalachian Trail and the triple crown of hiking. She was originally from Scotland but had lived in Alaska for the past 10 years.

We hiked together for the rest of the day and ended up at Spring Mountain Shelter. Upon arrival, we discovered what appeared to be a lunchbox-sized cooler and a bag of trash in the shelter. The cooler had some food items in it and a large butcher knife. The bag was a plastic bag from a local hospital, the type they give you to put clothing items in when you are discharged. The name was crossed out but it looked fairly recent. Fun Size checked the shelter log book and saw an entry from someone who stated they left to get medical help and was sorry for leaving the trash but would be back and feel free to eat the food.

Fun Size packed everything together, including the knife, and hung it up on the bear pole in front of the shelter. We joked that at least if some weirdo came back in the middle of the night looking for his stuff, we would hear him messing with the bear pole and would be ready for him. While I was at the hostel the night before, there was a southbound hiker staying there and he had told me that a guy came into the shelter the previous night after dark making a lot of noise. He got up at 5:30 am and told the southbounder that he was going for a walk and would be back to get his stuff. He said the guy was acting really weird. Obviously, he hadn't come back for his stuff yet.

I made sure I had my leg roller, a hard plastic rolling stick I carried to roll out my muscles every night, next to me as I laid down to sleep. If he did come back that night, I was ready to knock him upside the head if need be. Fortunately, the only intruders that night were the mice in the shelter.

By the time I woke up, ate breakfast, and packed up to leave, Fun Size was already hitting the trail. I hiked alone all day but did run into a couple of hikers who were doing a weekend hike and both recognized me from my YouTube page. It was really weird to be walking alone in the woods, in the middle of nowhere, and have someone approach you on the trail and recognize you. It was nice to take a short break and chat with the hikers and I enjoyed the company. After a few minutes, I continued to hike and eventually made it to a shelter only to discover Fun Size and two section hikers were already there.

It was nice to run into section hikers that were just out for the weekend because they usually had a lot of food with them and were always willing to share some with you. They would also usually build a fire and that was nice. I enjoyed having a campfire, but as a thru-hiker, you were usually too tired to collect wood and mess with a fire. Weekend hikers didn't mind sharing their fire with us as we sat around answering gear questions and telling stories of the trail.

Fun Size and I continued to hike to the same shelters for the next couple of days. Typically, she would get on the trail 15 or so minutes ahead of me and we would usually meet up with each other late in the day or at the end of the day at the shelter. We covered 15 1/2 miles to the Hogback Ridge Shelter and covered 20.7 miles the next day. It was my first 20-mile day and it felt good to do it. We ended up at the No Business Shelter where we ran into a section hiker from Australia and another northbounder named Old Soul.

Old Soul was an 18-year-old girl from Tennessee who started her hike back in November. She hiked for several weeks before going home for the holidays. She recently returned to where she left off and planned on going all the way. The weather was turning colder again but I was just 6 miles from Erwin, TN and was planning on staying at Uncle Johnny's Hostel the next day so I could resupply and wash clothes. After 28 days on the trail, I had traveled 337 miles and was feeling good.

While hiking the 6 miles to Erwin, I re-strained my right

foot. I had tweaked it in the Smokies but with the downhills I was doing as I descended to Erwin, the pain returned. It was where the front of my leg met my foot and as I continued to hike, it continued to hurt more. I made it to Uncle Johnny's and tried to doctor it up with some KT tape.

I pushed 17 miles the next day and my foot hurt for a while but then seemed to get better. It was always in the back of my mind that one single injury could end my hike. Quitting was not an option for me but in order to complete a thru-hike, a hiker has to have a certain amount of luck. One wrong step or one wrong move could mean the end of a dream. Since the hike began, I had been keeping a journal and I made sure I wrote in it every night before I went to sleep. On each journal page, I would put a tick mark to denote each time I had fallen on the trail. Every time I fell, there was always that brief moment when your heart would race, worried that you injured yourself to the point it would end your hike. The same was true for strains like the one I had in my right foot. I prayed it wasn't something that would get worse.

Fun Size, Old Soul, and myself wound up hiking together some over the next several days and stayed at the same shelters and hostels until we reached Roan Mountain. I was planning on meeting a few of my college classmates who came to Roan Mountain for the weekend to see me and do a little hiking with me. David Magee, the owner of The Station at 19e and the Doe River hostel hosted me and my buddies.

It was really good to see my classmates and it was a big morale booster for me. Chris, Norm, and Mitch not only hiked a day with me, but they also made sure I was resupplied and fed well all weekend. We all graduated from The Citadel in Charleston, SC and coming from a small military school, we were a tight-knit group. The camaraderie that exists between Citadel graduates is similar to the bond you create with other thru-hikers. There is a sense of loyalty and cooperation that does not exist in the "civilized" world. I knew my Citadel brothers would do anything for me and, in turn, I would do the same.

Although they were my classmates from college, we graduated 28 years before and usually only saw each other every 5 years at reunions. But when word got out that I was taking this hike, the support started to roll in. Phone calls, text messages, social media messages, and now a personal visit. My classmates had my back. The trail was teaching me who I could depend on and who I couldn't. The further I hiked from Springer Mountain, the further away I was from the life I once knew and some of the people I once knew.

I had an opportunity to hike 10 miles with my classmates and we had a good day to do it. The sun was shining and the air was crisp. We were dropped off 10 miles north and hiked southbound back towards Highway 19e. We passed Fun Size as she headed north and passed another hiker who was wearing shorts and had both shins bleeding. He apparently had to do some bushwhacking and plowed through some sticker bushes that sliced up his shins. While this was the first time I met him, both Old Soul and Fun Size had met him before. He was a recent Army retiree and was hiking north. Thanks to his unfortunate encounter with the bushes, he would become known as Scratch.

The next day was Sunday and my classmates were heading home. I did a short 8-mile section and returned to Doe River Hostel for one more night before I made the 72-mile push to Damascus, VA where I would resupply. The next day, I cranked out 22.7 miles and made it to Boots Off Hostel where I found Fun Size who had taken a day off as she was battling a cold. I met a section hiker named Banker and hiked a bit with him before arriving at Boots Off. He came rolling in after I had showered and he offered to take Fun Size and I to dinner. Not one to pass on free food, we all went into town and found a Mexican restaurant.

Over the next two days, Fun Size and I hiked 42 miles and made it all the way to the Virginia border and the town of Damascus. We had to walk through our first real snow shower as we had about an inch or so of accumulation. We were entering our fourth and longest state at 551 miles. In Damascus, we stayed at Woodchuck Hostel and resupplied before heading to Mt. Rogers and the Grayson Highlands.

CHAPTER 6

Revenge of the Smokies

The Grayson Highlands are known for having wild ponies, and as I hiked, I looked forward to seeing them. We were hiking in approximately 3-4 inches of snow and were climbing in elevation. Despite the cold and the snow, we made it 16 miles before getting to a shelter. Within minutes of arriving at the shelter, I had to remove my shoes that were soaked after walking through snow all day and pulled off my wet socks. I quickly grabbed a dry pair of socks from my bag and placed them on my feet. I then pulled the down booties out of my bag and placed them on my feet. Both Fun Size and myself got into our sleeping bags and laid in the shelter allowing our feet to thaw out and stop hurting from being cold. We made sure the laces on our shoes were untied and loosened so that they would be easier to put on in the morning.

When morning arrived, it was difficult to emerge from my quilt. I dreaded leaving my warm bag and exposing myself to the frigid air. While Fun Size heated up water for her coffee, I slowly emerged from my quilt. I grabbed my trail runners and attempted to put them on my feet but realized they were frozen solid. I pushed my dry, warm feet into the ice-cold frozen shoes. As I put one shoe on and then the other, I could feel the warmth of my feet start to dissipate as the heat from my feet defrosted frozen shoes. When the shoes defrosted, my socks absorbed the water from the shoes. So much for dry socks and warm feet.

When we hiked that day, we were greeted with more snow as we climbed higher and higher. Near the top of Mt. Rogers, we arrived at the Thomas Knob Shelter. We debated whether we should stay the night there or push on to the next shelter. It was already 4 pm and the next shelter was 4 more miles. The snow ranged from 4 inches to nearly a foot in spots. Thomas Knob was about 1,000-ft higher in elevation which meant it would be colder, but the shelter was a large two-story shelter with a loft that was protected from the wind. The weather report was calling for more snow overnight and temperatures in the 20s. Since our feet were soaked and already starting to freeze, we decided to stop for the day.

Before we could start our feet warming ritual, two weekend hikers showed up and decided to stay downstairs while Fun Size, myself, and a new thru-hiker we met, Snail's Pace, decided to stay upstairs in the loft to avoid the wind. The selection of tree options to hang our food bags on were few and far between. With all the snow, cold temperatures, and prediction of more snow overnight, we all agreed to sleep with our food.

We ate our dinner and settled in for a long winter's nap. I woke up around 9:30 pm as I heard another hiker arrive downstairs. He had two dogs with him and, after several minutes, he got settled in and I drifted back to sleep. Around midnight, I was awakened by the sound of my food bag being manipulated. I turned on my headlamp and stared at the food bag that was sitting on the floor next to my head. I saw a tail sticking out from behind the bag and I took my hand and back slapped the bag.

As I struck the bag, a black and white weasel-looking creature jumped back away from the bag. I shined my light directly at it and my first thought was that it was a skunk. As I examined its appearance, I started to have second thoughts. It was not as fluffy as a skunk and the markings, while the correct colors, were different. It started to creep back towards my bag and I slapped the bag again and it retreated a few inches. I grabbed my rolling stick and waited for it to creep closer. When he got within striking range, I swung at the creature with the stick and he instinctively jumped back. When he did, he fell down the hole in the floor that contained the ladder leading down from the loft.

I heard him hit the bottom floor and startle the dogs that were sleeping below. The dogs' owner woke up and called out, "hey, there are dogs down here," thinking I was attempting to climb down the ladder to use the bathroom. "I am not coming down," I said, "I just knocked some kind of animal down there that was trying to get my food." Fun Size woke up and looked over at me and I told her what happened. Snail's Pace was fast asleep and snoring like a buzz saw, so there was no waking him up. I turned off my light and tried to go back to sleep.

Before I could fall back asleep, I heard some movement in the corner of the shelter behind my head. I turned my light back on and, sure enough, the creature was back again trying to slowly creep back towards me and my food bag. He did not seem to mind that I was shining my light right at him. I swung my stick at him a few more times and, eventually, he disappeared into the corner of the shelter.

This scenario played itself out a couple more times before the creature decided to give Fun Size a try. She woke up and grabbed her trekking pole and started to stab at the creature with her pole. She looked at me and asked, "What is it?" and I replied that I didn't know but thought it was a skunk but the markings were different and he wasn't as fluffy as the skunks I have seen. We both wondered why he didn't bother Snail's Pace considering he had a lot more food than we did, including 3 lbs of chocolate. It then occurred to me that he was snoring so damn loud that the poor thing was probably scared to go near him.

Finally, around 3:30 am, Snail's Pace's snoring had subsided and, sure enough, I heard something messing with one of his food bags. I turned on my light and it was by Snail's Pace, trying to get some food. I called out to Snail's Pace and he woke up. Fun Size and I told him what was going on and he grabbed his trekking pole and chased the creature into the opposite corner and started to jab at it with his pole. "He is trapped and just sitting there," he said as he thrust his pole at the creature. "He is just letting me hit him, I feel kinda bad!" Just then, I could detect the faint but familiar smell. "It's a freaking skunk!" I exclaimed and just as I did, Fun Size chimed in, "I smell him!"

Fortunately, he was backed into the far corner of the shelter and when he sprayed, it sprayed into the corner and not out into the center of the shelter. Snail's Pace retreated back to his sleeping bag and we all laid back down and tried to go to sleep and prayed the skunk had decided to give up on his attempt to score some food. For the rest of the night, he left us alone and I was grateful I survived without getting sprayed.

When the nighttime lifted and the morning light started to invade the shelter through the windows on each side, everyone began to stir around. It had been a long night and we were all a little tired from the battle with the skunk. We packed up our stuff and discussed the plan for the day. They were calling for a little snow today and several more inches the next day. We were still a couple of days away from our next resupply but I had a problem. Hiking the last two days in snow left me with only one pair of dry socks as my other two were still wet from the previous two days.

We befriended the hiker with the two dogs and found out he was from Ohio and had driven here to do a little hiking. After the cold weather last night and the forecast for more, he was thinking about hiking back to his car and driving somewhere else to hike. Somewhere with better weather. His car was at Massey Gap where he parked it last night before hiking the 3 1/2 miles south to the shelter. We were going to pass right by the turn off for Massey Gap as we headed north and we asked him if he would give us a ride to somewhere we could stay until the weather passed.

He agreed to do so and we decided that the best option was to head back to Damascus. We could try to stay at Woodchuck's again for the night and probably take a zero the next day since it was going to snow again. We could then figure out what we needed to do and surmised it would be easier to get a shuttle back to the trail from Damascus.

We all headed out and started hiking as the wind was blowing and the snow was falling. We were hiking over open fields so we had no protection from the wind and strained to find the small wooded posts that marked the trail. You never realize how hard it can be to stay on the trail until you are hiking in a field that has 4-6 inches of freshly fallen snow on it. The newly fallen snow covered up not only the indention where the trail was, but it covered up the footprints from the day before. The few places where there was a small wooden post to help mark the trail, the blazes were white and the posts were covered with snow.

As we hiked and tried not to lose the trail, I thought back to the Smokies and the relatively mild weather I experienced there. I definitely was paying the price for having decent weather in the Smokies. We continued to hike and came across some ponies and stopped to take some pictures with them. As cool as it was to see the ponies, all I could think about was getting to the gap and getting in the car. I was following Snail's Pace, and every so often, I got a whiff of the skunk. Apparently, Snail's Pace did not escape untouched by our furry visitor the night before. Fortunately, he was the only one that took a hit.

We finally made it to Massey Gap and followed our newly found trail angel and his dogs to his car in the parking lot. He had an SUV and we packed four hikers, two dogs, and all our gear in his vehicle. As we rode down the mountain, I thought how lucky we were to be in a warm vehicle heading to town where we could dry out and have a warm place to stay for the night. If Fun Size and I would have pushed on the night before, we never would have met our trail angel and not be heading to town. The trail works in mysterious ways. Before starting my hike, I heard the phrase, "the trail will provide." I was experiencing that first hand. It seemed that every time I needed something, a trail angel would appear or some trail magic would appear and give me what I needed.

I did not want to have to stop hiking for the day and potentially take a zero-day tomorrow, but I needed to do what I needed to do in order to be safe. Laine was set to come and see me in less than two weeks and I needed to get to Daleville, VA to meet her. Even though this could set me back, I wanted to get dried out and then I could look at my guidebook and figure out what to do.

We arrived at Woodchuck's and, fortunately, he had room. Snail's Pace had to hang some of his stuff outside to air out the skunk smell but Fun Size and I were spared. As we were getting settled in, more and more calls came in from other hikers who were on their way into Damascus and looking to stay at Woodchuck's to wait out the storm just like we were about to do. Before the day was over, it was a full house. A lot of northbounders had shown up to include Zack and his dog, Tank.

I called Laine and told her where I was and that I planned on taking a zero the next day. Along with her help, we came up with a plan that would help me get to Daleville in time to meet her. One of my wife's relatives had section hiked the entire AT over a several-year period and was currently retired. We had spoken several times before I started the trail and once after the

Smokies. He and his wife had been wanting to come and help me slack-pack for a few days and they just happened to contact Laine. They were going to travel to Damascus and take us back to where we came off the trail and slack-pack us for a couple of days. This would allow us to hike without all our food and a few other items and let us get picked up at the end of each day, dry out in a hotel, and eat a good dinner and breakfast.

After showering and washing my clothes, I spent the rest of the day relaxing and socializing with all the hikers that had arrived. The next day, several of us did a small resupply in town and then hung out for the rest of the day. Later that night, a northbound hiker named Overhill arrived and I had a chance to talk to him. He was an Eagle Scout from California and had hiked the PCT previously. He was attempting to hike the AT in 100 days and, so far, was making good time. My relatives, Emmett and Sherrie, called me early in the evening and had gotten a hotel room about 30 minutes away. They planned to come and get me the next morning and invited Fun Size to come along since we had been hiking together.

Several times earlier in my hike, Emmett and Sherrie tried to work out a time to come and see me. They wanted to help me when I needed it and this was an opportune time. They arrived right on time at 7 am and Fun Size and I got in their truck and started heading back to the trail. As we rode back to Grayson Highlands State Park, the snow started to fall. The higher we climbed, the more the snow started to fall. We arrived at the parking lot and I took a deep breath and stepped out of the truck and into the snow.

Emmett and Sherrie planned to meet us about 9 miles up the trail at a road crossing and were going to have some food for us. Fun Size and I headed off out of the parking lot and back on the trail. Knowing that we would be able to stop for lunch and take a break in a vehicle really helped my morale and we pushed through the snow and started to cover some ground. A few miles into the hike, we came across the Wise Shelter and noticed some footprints leading north from the shelter. Since it had snowed the night before, we knew that the prints were freshly made by whoever stayed at the shelter the night before. We walked over to the shelter and Fun Size found the shelter log and opened it up to see if we could see who stayed there the previous night.

As she opened the book, she looked at the last entry. It was Old Soul! We figured she was behind us when we left the trail the other day and we were right. Since it was fairly early in the morning, we figured we could probably catch up with her if we pushed a bit. All we had to do was follow her footsteps and get moving. As we hiked, we talked about how tough she was to have hiked and camped alone the previous day and night. It wasn't long before we saw her up ahead on the trail and yelled out to her. We told her what we were doing and that it was our plan to stay in a hotel for the next two nights. I told her she needed to stick with us and we could cover some good miles over the next couple of days.

The terrain had some moderate climbing but some decent downhills also. While the snow on the trail was deep enough to ensure that our feet remained wet, as long as we kept moving, my feet would stay warm enough not to freeze. The biggest problem was the rhododendrons. Most of the trail was surrounded by them on both sides and it gave the trail a tunnel effect. With all the snow that had fallen, the branches of the rhododendrons were covered with snow and weighed down so much that the branches bent down, blocking the path. As we hiked, the lead person had to slap at the branches with their trekking pole so it would knock off the snow and the branches would spring back up and unblock the path. When this was done, however, the lead person would be showered with the cold wet snow as it was knocked off the branches. Every 30 minutes or so, we would take turns hiking the lead and everyone did their fair share of clearing a path through the trail.

When we got to the road crossing to meet Emmett and Sherrie, they were already there waiting on us. We introduced Old Soul to them and Sherrie started handing us food and drinks while we pulled off our packs and took a break. After eating and fueling up, we headed back out and planned to meet them at another road crossing at the end of the day so we could head to town and find a hotel. We were able to get to Dickey Gap by 5 pm and got a hotel in Marion. The plan was to use that hotel as a home base for two nights while Emmett and Sherrie shuttled us back and forth from the trail.

We covered 17.4 miles the first day and busted out a 25.5-mile day the next. Definitely my longest mileage day thus far and I had to hike through snow to do it. We were able to cover the first 14 or so miles before meeting Emmett and Sherrie just past the Partnership Shelter where they were waiting for us with some pizza for lunch. After eating, Emmett threw on his day pack and decided to join us for the next 11 miles we planned on covering by dinner. All four of us told Sherrie we would see her in a few hours and we headed on our way.

After meeting back up with Sherrie at the end of the day, we all went to The Barn Restaurant and celebrated a long day with some really good cheeseburgers and fries. Back at the hotel, I dried out my clothes and shoes and repacked my gear for the next day. We would be checking out of the hotel and saying goodbye to Emmett and Sherrie before pushing north on our way to Daleville where I would meet Laine in a week and a half. The last two days were cold and snowy but the hotel and food we were able to enjoy, thanks to Emmett and Sherrie, allowed us to cover 43 miles in some tough conditions. Once again, the path provided what we needed when we needed it the most. I was sitting at mile 545.2 after 43 days. While I felt like the worst was over and I was able to make it through some tough weather conditions, I was not prepared for the next challenge I

Glenn Justis

would face.

CHAPTER 7

It Can Always Get Worse

After getting some sleep and making sure all my gear was dry, I packed up and prepared to meet everyone for breakfast. Being able to eat some good food and get out of the elements for the last several nights really helped allow me to tolerate the cold and snow we faced over the last five days. There was no snow in the forecast but there was still plenty of snow on the ground. Being some of the first NOBOs for the season, we would have to break trail. It was mid-March, so winter wasn't over yet but I hoped that spring was on its way.

After eating some breakfast and bidding farewell to our trail angels, Emmett and Sherrie, Fun Size, Old Soul, and myself headed out of Atkins and back into the snowy mountains. It was in the low 20s and windy. We had several big ups for the day but I was really looking forward to passing the 1/4-way mark today. We got to the marker and all of us took a picture in front of the sign. Being able to think that I hiked a quarter of the trail gave me some motivation. As we hiked, we hit some snow drifts 2 feet deep and it was slow going. Several times during the day, we had to try to figure out which way the trail was heading as it was very difficult to see the trail and the blazes. Eventually, we made it to Knot Maul Shelter and bedded down for the night.

The next day was March 15th and we headed out on the

snowy trail. I was leading the group. I watched each step I took to make sure I had solid footing as my feet sunk into the crunchy white snow. The weather report was calling for the temperatures to be above freezing today. It might reach the 50s and only get down into the 40s in the evening. I was hoping that would help with the snow and allow some of it to melt. As I looked down, I suddenly heard Fun Size calmly say "bear" from behind. Before I could look up, she reiterated it a little more forcefully. I stopped dead in my tracks and looked ahead in the trail quick enough to see a tiny black bear cub cross the trail about 100 feet in front of me and start to climb a tree right next to the trail. We scanned the landscape looking for Momma.

While black bears will typically flee upon the sight of a human being, it is not a good idea to get in between a cub and their momma. Since the cub was in a tree right on the side of the trail, we would have to pass just below where he was and we did not want to be that close. We could not see any sign of Momma. The left side of the trail sloped down steeply as we were hiking on the west side of the mountain. There was no way to go around the tree on that side. On the right side was a steep incline. Fortunately, the incline was not too high and we decided to go up the incline before passing the area of the trail where the cub was located. That would give us a bird's eye view to see if we could see Momma. When we got on top of the incline, there still was no sign of Momma so we quickly semi-bushwhacked along the ridge until we passed the bear then descended the incline and returned to the trail. So much for bears hibernating in the winter, I thought. As I later would find out, black bears really do not hibernate. They typically become more lethargic and stick close to the den when the weather is cold. Fortunately for us, we did not have to see Momma.

We began the long climb heading towards Chestnut Knob Shelter. The shelter sat atop Chestnut Knob and was an old fire warden's cabin which had been converted to an enclosed trail shelter that included room for 8 campers. The shelter was at the 9-mile mark for the day and we arrived mid-afternoon. We walked inside the cabin to take a break from the wind and to have a snack before heading back out on the trail. Our plan was to hike another 11 miles to the Jenkins Shelter, but first, it was time to re-group and take a break.

I checked my phone to see our progress and realized that I had some decent cell service, so I decided to call Laine. After a couple of rings, Laine's familiar voice answered and I greeted her. I told her we were taking a break in a shelter and I just wanted to say hi. "I need to tell you something and you are going to be upset," she stated. At that moment, I could tell something was wrong. Being at the top of a snow-covered mountain literally hundreds of miles from home was not a good place to be when hearing my wife say those words. "What's wrong?" I inquired, wanting her to tell me as soon as possible in order to relieve the uneasy feeling that immediately started to accumulate in my stomach. "Cotter died," she said with a sense of utter loss in her voice. Cotter was one of my scouts. The same scout that, 6 years earlier, suggested we hike the Grand Canyon. He was 17 years old and was the same age as my son. They had grown up together and he joined our Cub Scout Pack when he was 7 years old.

"What happened?" I asked. She began to tell me about how he was playing basketball in his driveway with some friends after school the day before and was not feeling well. Eventually, he was taken to the hospital and passed away from an aortic dissection. As she was telling me what happened, I was only half listening. I thought about Cotter and his family and what they were going through. I thought about all the other scouts and I thought about Joe. I wondered how they were dealing with losing one of their friends.

Laine had been worried that I would see it on social media before she could talk to me. When I got to the cabin, something just told me to check my phone and see if I had service to call home. I knew there was nothing I could do at that moment and I was still trying to process what had transpired. When I hung up the phone with Laine, I told Fun Size and Old Soul what happened. We chatted some about Cotter and then finished our snacks and decided to hit the trail. I could not do anything at that moment to help, so I decided to just keep pushing north.

As we continued hiking, I thought about Cotter. The trail was a lot of ridge walking and there was a lot of snow. At times, the drifts were up to my knees and we took turns breaking trail. It was not easy going but I just kept reminding myself that what I was experiencing was nothing compared to the events back home. My thoughts were not on the trail but with those individuals back at home. With the drifts we were having to trudge through, it was obvious that it would be after dark before we reached the shelter. My morale was not good and I really did not want to keep going. I realized that even though I was still trying to process the news I had received, it was important for me to keep pushing north. Fortunately, the trail provided me with two other thru-hikers to help motivate me when I needed it most. Again, the trail provided me what I needed.

We kept switching positions and taking turns leading and breaking trail. Slowly, the miles added up and the sun started to set. As the light began to fade and the darkness crept in, we pulled out our headlights and turned them on. Fun Size took the lead and I brought up the rear behind Old Soul. Eventually, around 8:30 pm, we pulled into Jenkins Shelter. The shelter was empty and so was the campsite. Luckily, it was only going to get down into the mid-40s overnight and that fact gave me something to be grateful for after a long and difficult day. None of us were in the mood to cook so we set up our sleeping bags and sat around eating whatever food we had in our bags that didn't need to be cooked. It was supposed to be sunny and in the 50s tomorrow and that would help melt some of the snow. It was a tough day but I was safe in a shelter. We hiked 20 miles in the snow today and into the night. I lost one of my scouts. A young man who had his whole life in front of him and a great family around him. Despite all that, I was grateful to be where I was and grateful that I had this opportunity. The trail never gets easier, you just do more miles.

It was a blessing not to have to sleep in sub-freezing temperatures for a night and I thanked my newest trail angel for looking out for me and providing me a respite from the cold. The further I traveled along the trail, the more I learned to appreciate the simple things in life. None of us are guaranteed the next day and it is important to live each day to the fullest. I made a commitment to my family, friends, scouts and, most importantly, to myself. As I packed up the next morning and got back on the trail, I spent most of the day in my own thoughts. I thought about all the adventures I had done with my scouts and how I got as much from those experiences as the scouts did.

I was a week away from seeing Laine but had a lot of miles to cover beforehand. I was able to call Laine as I was hiking. It was her birthday and I was able to hike and talk for over thirty minutes. It was really good to be able to speak with her on her birthday and get to talk to her for a long time. The trail was pretty easy and the snow was melting. There was a restaurant we were supposed to hike right past and we prayed it would be open when we got there around lunchtime. Since it was mid-March, they were still on a limited schedule.

When we got to the restaurant, it was a beautiful sight to see the open sign in the window. Old Soul and I pulled off our packs and left them outside the front door right next to Fun Size's pack who had left camp before us and was already inside. I ordered a big cheeseburger with fries and washed it all down with a couple of sodas. For dessert, I had some ice cream and purchased a couple of more sodas to pack out.

Eventually, we lifted our full bellies out of the booth and headed back onto the trail to finish the last 2.2 miles for the day. As usual, the trail made sure to throw in a steep 500-foot climb right before we got to the shelter but having had a great lunch and knowing I had a soda to drink with my dinner that evening gave me the motivation to push hard and get to camp. As luck would have it, I had cell service and was able to call Laine again. She was really happy to hear from me twice in the same day, especially since it was her birthday. Last night was our weekly scout meeting and the church where we meet provided a pastor to meet with our scouts and parents to help them deal with the loss of Cotter. Laine also told me that Cotter had previously finished all his merit badges he needed to complete for his Eagle Scout rank and was actually in the process of working on his Eagle Scout service project prior to his passing.

The finishing touches on his project were set to take place the next day and the scouts decided at the meeting that they would still meet to finish the project. Hearing this, I could not be more proud of my guys. Even though they were dealing with the death of their friend, they banded together to do the right thing and make sure the job Cotter started was going to get done. Laine told me that she spoke with our local council concerning Cotter's progress towards Eagle and they informed her that if the project was not complete, then he wouldn't be able to get his Eagle Scout rank. They did have another award called the Spirit of the Eagle Award that they awarded to scouts who pass prior to earning their Eagle Scout rank and he could be awarded that award.

Since the Eagle Scout service project requires a scout to "plan, develop, and give leadership to a service project that benefits your church, school, community..." it was my opinion that Cotter had satisfied the requirement. His project was to build and install a Gaga ball pit at the elementary school his Mom worked at as a school nurse. He planned and developed the entire project, including getting all the permissions, researching the pit designs, and ordering all the materials to build the pit. When it came time to stain and pre-assemble the materials, he recruited scouts and classmates to assist and he supervised the work. The only thing left to do was meet one final time to install the pit at the location.

As a Scoutmaster and Eagle Scout myself, it was clear to me that he completed the requirements to earn his Eagle rank. It was also clear that the Boy Scout Council did not know to what extent he had already proceeded with his project before passing. I told Laine not to worry, we would make sure Cotter got his Eagle and have a Court of Honor ceremony just like all the other Eagle Scouts from our troop even if I had to give him my own Eagle medal. For ten years, he came to the meetings and participated in the campouts and hikes. He served in several leadership positions within the troop, attended two National Scout Jamborees, and even attended Sea Base High Adventure Base. He was the type of scout and young man that you would expect to see wear that badge.

After speaking with Laine on the phone and eating a little dinner, through the woods came another hiker. As he approached the shelter, I could see that it was Overhill. It was good to see him again and we all chatted about the snow we encountered since leaving Damascus. Overhill was pushing big miles as he caught up to us after making up the 32 miles he was behind us when we first met him back at Woodchuck's. I told him about Cotter's death and it felt good to talk with a fellow Eagle Scout about what happened and what my scouts were going to do to honor their fellow scout. He agreed that Cotter deserved his Eagle and I told him I was going to do whatever it took to make sure it happened.

The next morning, we all got up and went through our morning routines. Everyone had their own routine of eating and packing up and Overhill was the first to head out, followed by

Fun Size, me, and finally, Old Soul. We all hiked separately in the morning but I eventually ran into Fun Size and Overhill as they were taking a break near a road crossing. I was contemplating hiking a half mile down off trail to stop at Trent's Grocery to grab a drink and something to eat. Overhill was thinking the same thing so we headed off together while Fun Size kept pushing north. It was a short road walk to the store and I was able to get a hot dog and a cold soda. After eating, we hiked back up the road to the trail and pushed on. While we hiked, Overhill and I talked about scouts and many other topics. We hiked and talked and the miles passed by and so did the time. Again, the trail provided me what I needed when I needed it. Having someone to talk to about Cotter and scouting allowed me to go through the mourning process. I did not feel alone on the trail having a fellow Eagle to confide in.

We were all planning on hiking 24 miles to the Wapiti Shelter and, late in the afternoon, we caught up to Fun Size and, eventually, Old Soul caught up to all of us. The skies were clouding up and we were trying to beat the impending storm to the shelter. As the clouds rolled in and thunder started to fill the sky, we all picked up the pace. It can be a little unsettling when you hear all the thunder and realize you are exposed to the elements and carrying two metal hiking poles in your hands. Fun Size was working on her third long-distance trail and had experienced bears, mountain lions, and all sorts of other dangers but made it clear that hiking in a thunderstorm was her biggest fear.

We were 3/10's of a mile from the shelter when the rain started to fall. It seemed like with each step, the rain increased in intensity and so did the thunder and lightning. We started to jog in an effort to get to the shelter as quickly as possible. As I ran, I kept my eyes on the trail in front of me and hoped I would not take a misstep and fall flat on my face. As the rain fell down on me, I took the spur trail to the shelter and raced into the shelter and out of the rain. Everyone followed and we all celebrated as we escaped the rain and lightning. Unfortunately, we were all pretty soaked but I knew I had some dry clothes in my bag. The weather was calling for on and off storms all night but we were just happy we had made it without too much trouble. We were all planning on hiking 17 miles into Pearisburg, VA tomorrow and would have a chance to stay at a hostel and get our stuff all dried out.

The Wapiti Shelter has been rumored to be haunted after two people were murdered there years before. Reading the shelter log book and comments on Guthooks, there are conflicting stories about whether the murders happened at this exact shelter or the previous Wapiti Shelter that was located nearby but eventually torn down and replaced with this one. Several individuals have reported strange occurrences at the shelter and we all talked about the rumors as we cooked our dinners and got ready to go to sleep. I thought to myself that not only did I have to worry about mice, now I had to worry about ghosts. After a 24-mile day and running through a thunderstorm, I was just happy that I was warm and dry and heading into town the next day.

I had some service on my phone and even had some LTE service. I was able to check social media and Laine shared with me some pictures from the Eagle Scout service project that our scouts finished in honor of their fellow scout. Seeing the pictures of my scouts pulling together and completing this project made me feel proud. I knew that I needed to keep pushing north on the trail as my scouts would not want me to quit. If they could finish this project while mourning the loss of their friend, I could keep hiking.

I wrote a message to my scouts and was able to text it to Laine. I asked her to send an email out to the troop on my behalf and include the message:

"Scouts,

I know it has been a difficult few days with the passing of our friend and fellow scout Cotter. It has been my experience and my belief that God puts people in our lives for a reason. Sometimes they are with us a long time and sometimes they are with us a brief time. Either way, they enrich our lives for the better and Cotter definitely enriched our lives.

While it has been difficult for me to be hundreds of miles away and not there to help comfort everyone, I have come to realize that the foundation myself and the other adult leaders have tried to instill in all of you scouts has taken hold. Seeing the pictures of the Eagle project and seeing the scouts come together to finish the work started by Cotter, let me know that you scouts have learned the lessons the Scout Oath and Law are there to teach. It also tells me that when you stick together as fellow scouts, you can get through any difficult situation. That is why I have always tried to challenge you guys with things such as 77 mile hikes in the cold or other such difficult tasks. Cotter's passing is another difficult challenge we face but based on how you have handled past challenges I have no doubt my scouts will persevere.

The older scouts have proven they are capable of running the Troop and helping the younger ones when needed. Eagle Scouts, it is time to fulfill the Eagle Scout Promise you took and spring into action. Troop 2 was created to be a Troop run by boys for the benefit of the boys. Cotter was the Scout who suggested going to the Grand Canyon and it became a reality. We owe it to him to all live our lives by the Scout Oath and Law and let that guide us in everything we do.

Take care of each other and I will see you all after I hike to Maine.

Yours in Scouting,
Mr. Glenn"

I felt helpless sitting in a shelter in Virginia while my scouts and Cotter's family were dealing with his loss. I believed I needed to be home where I could help but I also knew that I needed to complete this trail. I did not know what to do but from my experience on the trail so far, I knew the answer would be revealed to me when the time was right.

CHAPTER 8

Winter Be Gone

After a night of on and off thunderstorms, the rain had stopped by the morning. Overhill and Fun Size headed out early from the shelter as Old Soul and myself finished breakfast and packed up our gear. I took my time and was the last one to leave the shelter. As I hiked, I listened to music on my iPod and enjoyed the nice weather as the sun came out and the temperatures were moderate. I hiked most of the morning by myself and spent the time just thinking. I was excited to get to town but was even more excited that I wasn't having to hike in two feet of snow. As usual, the trail had its fair share of ups and downs but nothing too bad. Old Soul only had a 15-minute head start on me so I knew that if I walked fast, I could catch up with her. Before lunch, I did catch up with her and we hiked the rest of the way into Pearisburg.

Hiking into town, we ran into Overhill who asked us where the hostel was located. He had already eaten some lunch so we gave him the address from the guidebook and headed to Dairy Queen for a late lunch before going to the hostel. There is something glorious about walking into a fast food restaurant after you have spent several days on the trail. I ordered the largest bacon cheeseburger they had with some fries and a large root beer. I was starting to get my hiker hunger and it was a weird feeling to order the biggest thing on the menu knowing that not only could I easily finish it, but I would also burn up the calories in no time and be hungry just a couple of hours later.

We walked across town to Angel's Rest Hostel and checked into the bunkhouse where Fun Size and Overhill were already located. We ran into Handy, the hiker we met back at Woodchuck's Hostel in Damascus, and learned he was working at Angel's Rest. The bunkhouse was a converted garage that included bunk beds, heat, and loaner clothes we could wear while washing our clothes. There was a nice double-wide trailer on the property that had a couple of private rooms, a living room for all to share and a kitchen. For the rest of the evening, we all hung out and watched a movie while ordering pizza and meatball subs from a local delivery place.

I was 637 miles in after 48 days and I was starting to get excited about seeing Laine in a few days. It had been over a month since I saw her and I had hiked through some crazy weather. Fun Size, Old Soul, and myself were all planning to continue to hike together until I met Laine. Old Soul was scheduled to leave the trail and catch a bus back to Nashville as she was going to be taking three weeks off to go home for Easter. Laine offered to take her to the bus station in Roanoke and Fun Size was planning on meeting an old PCT friend she knew in a few weeks, so she was going to push forward while I took a zero with Laine.

Over the next two days, we covered 45 miles as we continued to push hard to get to Catawba to meet Laine later in the week. Overhill wound up hiking a little further than us as he continued to push big miles, trying to hit his 100-day goal. Eventually, we wound up at the Server Hollow Shelter. The shelter was large with a beautiful covered porch and a picnic table. Definitely the nicest shelter I had seen on the trail thus far. We got set up and then cooked and ate dinner. It started raining and according to the weather report, the rain would turn to sleet and snow as the temperature dropped during the night. As I drifted off to sleep, I could hear the rain ease off as the temperature dropped.

When I woke up the next morning, I lifted my head and peered out of the shelter. Due to the porch, I could not see the ground but I could see the trees and their branches. It appeared that the branches were covered with about 2-3 inches of snow, which wasn't a good sign. After working my warm feet into my frozen solid shoes, I stepped out of the shelter to walk to the privy. Apparently, the weather report had been updated slightly since the other night when I checked it in Pearisburg. Instead of an inch of snow accumulation, it appeared we had at least 8 inches of accumulation overnight. The plan was to hike 16 miles and I knew it was going to be a challenging day. By the time we all ate breakfast, filtered some water, and got packed up, it was after 10 am. We started the nearly half-a-mile climb out of the shelter and finally reconnected with the AT. The first half of the hike was mostly some ridge walking and a big down but we soon learned that it was not going to be easy

The snow was knee deep in some spots and if that was not enough, there were rocks under the snow and they were icy in spots. Old Soul led the way and blazed the trail until she got tired and then Fun Size and I would take turns breaking trail. It was slow going and treacherous. Time after time, I would place my foot down and would wind up slipping and falling. Throughout the first 6 miles, I fell 12 times. We came across the Niday Shelter and stopped to take a break. As I looked into the shelter, I saw three Gatorades sitting there and a note stating, "Save one for the Scoutmaster." I yelled out to the others and we all grabbed a drink. Trail magic from one of my YouTube subscribers and it was a nice treat after 5 hours of slow going.

We looked at Guthooks and tried to come up with a game plan. It was after 3 pm and we were still about 10 miles from the next shelter. We needed to decide if we should push on or stay where we were. Looking at Guthooks, there was a road 1.5 miles ahead and we wondered if the road was clear and what type of traffic we might encounter at the road. If the road was clear, we might be able to flag down a car and get a ride into town and a hotel for the night. Laine was already driving to Greenville, SC to meet up with her Mom who was going to make the drive with Laine to see me the next day. If we could get to a town, they could meet us in town the next day. If the road was not open, we could always camp there or hike back to this shelter and spend the night.

We decided to risk it and pray the road was open and we could catch a hitch. We did not know how close we were to a town, but if there was a road, there had to be a town somewhere. We saddled our packs and headed back on the trail and hiked the 1 1/2 miles to VA Route 621. We arrived at the road and saw that it was plowed and clear. Fun Size and Old Soul searched up and down the road waiting for someone to come along while I checked my phone to see if I had service. I had a couple of bars and tried to call Laine. After a couple of rings, I heard Laine's voice. I told her we were going to try to get a hitch into town and would call her and let her know. While I was speaking with her, a pick-up truck approached us and the girls flagged down the truck which pulled over.

In the truck was a husband and wife named Maurice and Beth and their German Shepherd named Rex. They were on their way to Blacksburg to retrieve their cat from the vet. We explained our situation and asked if they could drop us off at a hotel. They agreed and we threw our packs in the bed of the truck and squeezed in the extra cab while Rex sat up front with his owners. We were about 15 miles from the nearest town and Maurice knew of a Microtel in Christiansburg that had reasonable rates. We exchanged stories with our trail angels and before long, we were pulling up to the hotel. As we gathered our packs, we thanked our trail angels for helping us out.

After getting a couple of rooms, we retreated to our rooms and I called Laine to let her know where we were. She was almost at Greenville and she decided to pick up her Mom and head straight to where we were and stay with me at the hotel that night. It was Wednesday and she was planning on staying until Sunday or Monday so we decided to figure out a hiking plan when she got here.

After getting settled in, I met Fun Size and Old Soul and we walked a few blocks to the KFC so we could get some dinner. It was starting to snow again and as I sat eating my dinner, I thought about where I was just a few hours earlier. I thought about standing at the shelter trying to figure out what we were going to do as I shivered from the cold. I thought about the 12 times I fell on the ice and rocks. I thought about the constant pain in my fingers and toes as the wet snow covered my shoes and gloves. As I thought about all of that, I also thought about how good it felt to be sitting in the restaurant while I was warming my belly with mashed potatoes, gravy, macaroni and cheese, fried chicken, and warm buttermilk biscuits. I had a warm bed and all the amenities waiting for me back at the hotel and, best of all, I was going to see Laine in just a few hours. The trail provided. I went from feeling like I was in a dire situation out in the cold snow to being safe and warm and about to see my wife. No matter how bad it gets on the trail, you are never more than a few hours from turning the situation around.

After eating, we walked back in the snow to the hotel. We looked at the guide to figure out our hiking plan for the next few days. Old Soul needed to be in Roanoke by 5 pm on Friday, so we planned on slackpacking 7.5 miles on Thursday and almost 14 miles on Friday. The snow was supposed to stop and the next two days would be sunny and above freezing. Hopefully that would allow some of the snow to melt.

When talking with Laine earlier in the week, she told me that there was going to be a memorial for Cotter on Saturday. Over the last couple of days, Cotter was on my mind a lot and I tried to figure out a way to be able to attend the memorial. As I checked the upcoming weather forecast for the next few days,

Walking to Maine

we were expecting more snow on Saturday. I was already planning on taking a zero-day on Saturday and the temperatures on Sunday were supposed to get up into the 50s. Since we were only 4 1/2-5 hrs from home, we could drop off Old Soul in Roanoke Friday afternoon and drive part of the way home and get a hotel Friday night. On Saturday, the memorial was not until 5 pm so we could be home by noon and have plenty of time to get ready for the memorial. Then we could drive back to Virginia on Sunday and get back on the trail on Monday. I would have to take a double zero but with the snow on Saturday, taking Sunday off would allow for some of that snow to melt before I had to hit the trail again. Again, the trail was providing. I wanted and needed to be there at that memorial and it seemed like the weather and trail conditions were trying to let me know it was the right thing to do.

I showered and relaxed as best I could while waiting for Laine to arrive. As she got closer, she would text me updates. A few minutes prior to her arrival, I went down to the lobby and waited for her. When I saw their vehicle pull up, I went outside into the cold and gave her a big hug and kiss. It was great to see her and be able to hold her again. Twelve hours earlier, I was in the frigid cold air packing up my stuff and getting ready to hike in the snow. Now, I was in a hotel with my wife. It was incredible to see how circumstances could change that drastically in such a short period of time.

In the morning, we all met for breakfast and loaded into the car so Laine could drive us back to the trail. We planned on hiking 7.5 miles and be done in time for lunch. Laine and her Mom, Judy, dropped us off and planned on meeting us in a few hours. Even though there was snow on the trail, it wasn't too bad and we did not have to slug our way through any big drifts. We worked our way up Brush Mountain and came to the spur trail that led to the Audie Murphy Monument. Audie Murphy, Medal of Honor recipient and one of the most decorated WWII vet-

103

erans, died in a plane crash at this location. We walked up the short spur trail and paid our respects at the monument. After taking a short break, we headed back to the AT and back down the northside of the mountain. Within minutes of arriving at the road, Laine and Judy pulled up and took us back to the hotel to relax before going to The Homeplace Restaurant in Catawba for dinner.

On Friday, we got up early and ate breakfast before heading out to the trail. The plan was to head to Catawba and hike southbound 13.8 miles. We were going to be hiking Dragon's Tooth and from what we read about it, it would be a safer hike to go southbound, especially since it was likely to have a lot of ice and snow on the rocks. Even though we did hit snow and ice, it wasn't too bad as the temperatures the past two days were cold but they were in the 40s so it allowed some of the snow to melt. While hiking, we realized that Old Soul would be leaving the trail for a few weeks and I was going to be taking a double zero. While Fun Size and I might cross paths again, we would not see Old Soul again. Although it was sad to part ways and possibly not see each other again, we each had our own hike to hike and we were fortunate to have met each other when we did. I had no doubt in my mind that we were brought together by the trail. I do not know if I would have been able to deal with all the snow and other obstacles and trails if I had been alone. We complemented each other and supported each other but were all entering a new phase of our hikes.

As we emerged from the woods and approached the trailhead, Laine and Judy were waiting for us with some Chick-Fil-A for a late lunch. We ate our food and piled into the vehicle and headed back to Catawba so we could drop off Fun Size to continue her hike north. After that, we would head to Roanoke so Old Soul could catch her bus home and then we would head back to South Carolina. When we arrived at the parking lot at Catawba, we all said our goodbyes to Fun Size and wished her luck. The three of us had become a trail family or "tramily", as they are known on the trail, and we all wanted to see each other get to Maine and be able to touch the sign on the top of Katahdin. We watched as Fun Size crossed the road and started to climb back onto the trail. Next stop was Roanoke and the Greyhound Bus Station.

The drive to Roanoke did not take long and when we pulled up to the station, we said our goodbyes to Old Soul and wished her luck. I told her I would keep tabs on her and definitely could not wait to see her summit. It was sad to see them go but I knew that I still had two-thirds of the trail to go and I was sure I would meet many more individuals that I would come to know and consider family. We drove out of Roanoke and started the drive home.

We drove for a couple of hours and wound up finding a hotel in North Carolina to stop for the night. The next morning, we woke up bright and early and got back on the road. The only people who knew we were coming back home for the memorial were my son, Joe, and my Troop Committee Chairman. As we drove, Laine contacted Cotter's Mom and let her know that I was coming home for the weekend to attend the memorial and would head back to the trail the next day. She had requested someone from the troop speak at the memorial, so as Scoutmaster, I offered to do it. I had no idea what I was going to say but I jotted down some notes as Laine drove. I thought about all the things that I had been thinking about since I heard the news. Most importantly, I just wanted to be back with the troop and be there with them and Cotter's family.

As we turned off the interstate and drove the last few miles to the house, I sat and reflected about the last time I was home. It had been 55 days since I had been home and while it was nice to be back, it was for the wrong reason. I knew I needed to be with my troop but I also knew that my hike had to continue and that I needed to make sure I got to Maine. I had already been through some pretty cold and snowy weather and I knew that eventually spring would find me and things would get better. I was 709 miles into my journey, nearly 1/3 of the trail was complete. I was looking forward to seeing everyone before heading back out on the trail.

Arriving at home, I was greeted at the front door by my German Shepherd, Gunner. He was so excited to see me and I was excited to see him. He jumped up on me and whimpered as I hugged him and rubbed his belly. It was nice to get such a warm welcome. I wondered what he thought these last two months while I was gone. Whatever it was, I was home again for a little while and he at least knew I had not left for good.

After eating some lunch, I reorganized my pack and was able to get rid of a few things I did not need. As I was doing that, Joe came home and saw me for the first time since waving goodbye from the parking lot at Springer Mountain. He had been helping out on an Eagle Scout project for one of my other scouts. I had lost 26 lbs since the last time he had seen me and my beard was filling in and getting longer. It was good to see him and I started telling him about my adventure this far.

As the time grew closer to the memorial service, I showered and put on my scout uniform. We drove to the church and when I got out of my car, I saw some of my Scouts already waiting by the entrance to the church gymnasium where the service was going to be held. They were surprised but happy to see me. It was great to see all of the scouts and other friends but it was bittersweet. The gymnasium filled up as over 400 people showed up to pay their respects for Cotter.

As I sat there during the ceremony, I reflected back on my journey thus far and I thought about Cotter. Despite all of the hardships that I encountered on the trail, I knew that I was lucky to be on the trail and able to experience the journey I was on. I knew that I would be heading back to Virginia in the morning and back on the trail the next day. As I was sitting in the gymnasium, it was snowing back on the trail. I knew the snow would be waiting for me when I got back but that seemed like an insignificant concern when I thought about what Cotter's family was going through.

When it came time for me to speak, I rose from my seat. I walked up to the podium and pulled out the paper that contained the notes I had written down. I cleared my throat and began to speak. I spoke about how I had come to know Cotter when he joined my Cub Scout den in the second grade. He was a boy who clung to his mother's leg but grew into a young man who climbed up and down the Grand Canyon. He was ever so close to earning his Eagle Scout rank when he passed and I talked about what a person had to do to become one. As I went through the requirements, I made the case for why Cotter had earned his Eagle. He earned all the required merit badges, served in multiple leadership positions within the troop, and finally, he planned, developed, and gave leadership to a service project benefiting his community. I believed in my heart that he had earned the distinction, regardless of whether the Boy Scouts would officially recognize him with that honor.

After the service, the scouts and their families joined Cotter's family to have a bonfire at their home. It was nice to spend time with everyone and especially spend time with Cotter's family. I was glad that I had taken the time off the trail and returned for the service. While it was nice to be home, I knew that I had unfinished business awaiting me on the trail. I was still almost 1,500 miles from Katahdin and I wanted to keep pushing north. While I was returning to the trail without Old Soul and Fun Size, I had a new trail angel walking with me.

CHAPTER 9

Renewed Spirit

I sat in the passenger's seat and watched as we made our way back to Virginia. As I peered out the window, I looked at the mountains off in the distance. Even though it seemed like a long drive to get back to Christiansburg, it was an even longer walk. I sat and thought about the fact that I had walked more miles in the last two months than we were going to drive that day.

It is difficult to comprehend how long 2,190.9 miles really is. While I still had nearly 1,500 miles to hike, I just focused on how far I had come. Knowing that I had already walked 709 miles was something that amazed me. When I thought about the last two months and all the rough weather and terrain I endured, it amazed me even more. As time went on, however, it all became part of my daily life and my daily thoughts. The more I hiked, the more I became a hiker. Pain was a daily occurrence but it only served to let me know I was still alive. I created mental games that I would play with myself to help the time pass by and make the day seem to go by quicker. Eventually, the miles would disappear and I would arrive in the shelter each night. I would set up camp, cook and eat dinner, then settle down for the night only to wake up the next morning and repeat the entire process.

We returned to the hotel we stayed in just a few days before and went and got some dinner. After dinner, we retreated to the hotel room and I prepared my backpack for the next morning. In the morning, Laine would drive me back to the trailhead at Catawba and we would say goodbye again. I would not see her again for nearly 600 miles. I would have to finish Virginia, West Virginia, Maryland, and even Pennsylvania before I would see her again. As tough as the trail was, it was just as tough to say goodbye again.

After breakfast the next morning, we loaded my backpack in the car and headed to Catawba. We arrived at the trailhead parking lot and I prepared myself to say goodbye. I would need to hike all the way to the Delaware Water Gap in New Jersey before meeting back up with Laine. We said our goodbyes and I gave her a hug and a kiss before grabbing my trekking poles and heading out of the parking lot. I crossed the highway and headed up the stairs leading me into the woods. As I looked back down to the parking lot, I watched as Laine drove out of the parking lot and disappeared from my view.

I started my nearly 4-mile hike heading to McAfee Knob, the most photographed spot on the AT. As I climbed, I thought about the events of the last couple of weeks. With all the snow, the passing of Cotter, and the second visit with Laine, I was ready to turn the page and enter the next phase of my hike. Since Old Soul was back home for a few weeks and Fun Size stayed on the trail when I went home, I would be back by myself pushing north. My plan was to push 20 miles and get to Daleville where I would get a hotel room. As I got near the top of the climb to McAfee Knob, a couple of hikers passed me as they were descending. When I crested the top of the mountain, I saw the iconic ledge that I had seen a thousand times before in many photographs. The sun was shining and the view was incredible. There was still some snow on the ledge and throughout the surrounding area but it accented the landscape perfectly.

I hiked throughout the day and, as I did, I thought about

Laine. I tried to do the mileage math in my head as to when I would see her again. Delaware Water Gap was almost at mile marker 1,300 so that left me with nearly 600 miles to cover. I computed it would probably take me 4-5 weeks to get there. While that seemed like a long time away, I kept reminding myself that every day that passed was bringing me not only closer to Maine, but closer to spring. After spending the last few weeks dealing with the snow, I kept telling myself that, eventually, spring would arrive. At times, it seemed like it was never going to come.

Without having anyone to hike with, I spent more time listening to music and thinking about my hike. The more I hiked, the more snow on the ground started to disappear. I hiked with a renewed sense of purpose as I knew that as soon as I could put Virginia behind me, the states would come and go much quicker. Having the two days off from hiking gave me some needed rest and I was able to eat some good food.

After pushing 20 miles the first day, I followed that up with 18.5 miles and 23.4 the next day. After 58 days, I was just over 771 miles in and over 1/3 of the way to Katahdin. I was in a good groove and feeling good. Looking ahead on the trail, I was set to get to the James River and the longest footbridge on the AT. I was trying to figure out where my next resupply would be as I did not have enough food to make it to Waynesboro, VA and the start of Shenandoah National Park. There were a couple of towns prior to that but I would probably have to hitch into town. Normally, I would have already figured out what my next town/resupply stop would be but, for whatever reason, I just wasn't sure what I wanted to do, so I just kept on hiking.

I was descending the mountain leading to the James River bridge and I stopped at a stream and filtered water. The temperature had gotten up to 70 degrees, and as a result, I was drinking a lot of water. The trail turned to follow the bank of the river for a mile and as I hiked I could see the footbridge ahead and the parking lot on the south side of the bridge. I peered at the parking lot and saw what I thought was a food truck. I was dying for something to drink and started to pray that I would be able to get a drink when I crossed the bridge.

As I got closer to the bridge, I continued to try to make out the vehicle in the parking lot. Slowly, I got closer and the vehicle got bigger and clearer. Eventually, to my disappointment, I could tell that it was a utility truck and not a food truck. I reached the bridge and began the 1,000' walk across the bridge. I had seen others cross this bridge on YouTube and now I was crossing it. It was a good feeling. I looked across to the opposite end and could see the parking lot. Several cars were parked in the lot along with the utility truck. I prayed that maybe one of the cars contained a trail angel and I scanned the parking lot for any signs of life.

Suddenly, I saw a man get out of one of the cars as I was nearing the end of the bridge. As I climbed down from the bridge and approached the parking lot, the man approached and called out "Scoutmaster!" I felt a huge wave of relief come over me and happily responded to the man. He asked if I would like something to eat or drink and I answered, "absolutely." His name was Gadget and he directed me to the back of his vehicle where he opened the trunk, revealing an array of drinks and snacks. I quickly grabbed a Mountain Dew Code Red and drank it. After days of drinking nothing but water, soda never tasted so good. I helped myself to some snacks and chatted with Gadget. He was a subscriber on my YouTube page and had been following me and was hoping to run into me on the trail.

I explained to him how I was hoping I would run into someone so I could get a drink. After talking for a few minutes, he asked me where I was planning on camping for the night. I told him I was heading to the next shelter 1.4 miles up the trail. He offered to drive my pack to the road crossing 1/2 mile from the shelter and I agreed. I was able to fly up the nearly one mile of trail and when I got to the road crossing, he was there waiting on me. We chatted some more as I had another drink. He told me to take whatever I wanted and I started to add stuff to my pack. Again, he told me to take more drinks but my pack was stuffed pretty good. He told me he had his pack in the car and would be happy to pack some goodies in it and hike the 1/2 mile to the shelter with me.

Gadget shouldered his pack and we began hiking. In a few minutes, we arrived at the shelter and I threw off my pack. I pulled out my phone to check for a signal to call Laine and tell her I reached camp, but there was no signal. Gadget asked me if I wanted to use his phone and handed it to me. I called Laine and told her where I was and who was with me. After talking for a minute, I hung up and gave the phone back to Gadget. As we unpacked the food and drinks, we continued to chat. Eventually, Gadget wished me luck and headed back to the trail and his car.

As I unpacked my pack and set up camp, I could not help but think about the trail magic I had received. When I started hiking that morning, I was still unsure where or when I would be able to resupply. After meeting my trail angel, Gadget, I now not only had several sodas to enjoy tonight and tomorrow, I had gotten enough food from him to last me until Waynesboro. I took two of the sodas and placed them in the stream next to the shelter so that they would be nice and cold for me in the morning. I was alone at the shelter and would spend the night by myself. As I laid down to go to sleep that night, I once again experienced the trail providing me what I needed when I needed it. With enough food for three more days, my sights were set on my next town stop, Waynesboro and the entrance to Shenandoah National Park.

After a solid night's sleep, I woke up and packed and got ready for another day. While I was eating some breakfast, I spotted a hiker passing the shelter heading north and talking on his cell phone. By the time I headed out, the hiker had a 5-10-

minute head start on me. Eventually, I was able to catch up to him and it was Scratch. He was an officer in the Army and was about to retire from the Army and enter civilian life.

We hiked and talked, and I found out he was married and had a 4-year-old daughter. Between the fact we both had a wife and kids at home and the fact we both graduated from military schools, we had a lot in common. We talked and the miles just seemed to fly by. It was always nice to meet someone new on the trail as you would get to know them and also share your story with them. For a few hours, you would forget about your sore legs and feet and you would just concentrate on the conversation you were engaged in.

We took a few rest breaks, eating some food and drinking some water. We talked about the trail and discovered we both had the same approach to our hikes. While we enjoyed the trail and the beauty of it, we both wanted the challenge of the trail and we missed our families. We saw Maine as the way home and the way back to the families that we loved. While some people never want the trail to end, we were looking forward to the day we could climb Katahdin and board a plane to get back home to our families.

After hiking over 18 miles that day, we came across the shelter I planned on staying at for the night. Scratch planned on hiking on some as he was going to be meeting his family in a couple of days. We wished each other luck and went our separate ways. The trail brought us together that day and, surely, we would see each other again. I had been on the trail for exactly 60 days and was sitting at mile marker 806.

After a rainy night, I got on the trail and was immediately faced with a 2,700' climb out of the shelter. Fortunately, it did not rain that day and I was able to push the miles and before I knew it was rolling into the Priest Shelter after a 22.4-mile day. I met a section hiker and his teenage daughter who were from

Maryland and also spent the night with another section hiker named Stickman. It was Saturday and it was the night before Easter. I thought it was pretty cool that I would wake up on Easter morning in the Priest Shelter. The irony of the situation was not lost on me. I had two more days before getting to Waynesboro and getting a shower and some good food.

For the next two days, I hiked and as I got close to Waynesboro, I felt a twinge in my right shin and began to hobble a bit. Since I was close to getting to the road crossing to be picked up, I pushed on hoping that some rest that evening would help make it feel better. I got to the road at 4:45 pm and was picked up and taken into town to Stanimal's Hostel. After showering and starting some laundry, I walked to a local Italian restaurant and feasted on some lasagna and a beer. I made my way to the local Walmart to resupply and headed back to the hostel to grab some sleep and much-needed rest for my leg. The next day, I would start Shenandoah National Park.

CHAPTER 10

Shenandoah

Shenandoah National Park encompasses an area of nearly 200,000 acres and over 500 miles of hiking trails. Included in that is 101 miles of the Appalachian Trail. Skyline Drive is probably what the park is best known for and the AT crosses the road multiple times. The southern end of the park is near Waynesboro, and after a stay in town to resupply and recharge, I made my way back to the trail and back to the entrance of the park.

My right shin was still hurting from the day before as I made my way along the trail in the cold, dreary air. It was cloudy but the sun was supposed to eventually break through around lunchtime. The more I hiked, the more my leg started to hurt. At times, I had a slight limp in my step but I continued to push on. Having just been back on the trail for a week since seeing Laine, I was not inclined to take another zero so soon and try to rest the leg. I would just do my best to walk it off.

As I made my way up to the top of Calf Mountain, I pulled out my lunch for the day. I had a bagel with spam and cheese and since it was chilly on top of the mountain, I continued to hike while I ate. Not long after I started to eat, the sun began to break through the clouds and warmed me up. I also noticed that my leg was starting to hurt just a little bit less. It was as if my mind was just willing my body not to hurt anymore. I was planning on doing over 20 miles and my legs were just going to have to co-operate and carry me the distance.

I had decent cell service throughout the day and that was a tremendous boost to be able to call Laine several times and talk to her. Eventually, I made it to the Blackrock Shelter and there were several people already there. Since it was the first week in April, a lot of people were on spring break and they were out hiking in the park. I met a teacher and his wife from South Carolina and it was nice to talk with them. I was nearly 884 miles in and if all went according to plan, I would pass 900 miles the next day. And to top it off, my leg was not hurting anymore.

Each day, it seemed like the miles were starting to add up and I celebrated every time I reached another 50 or 100-mile milestone. The weather and temperatures were still up and down and I would go from having weather in the 50s to weather in the 20s. I planned on making my next town stop in Luray but I had to hike 38 miles in two days in order to get there. I set out to do a 24-mile day and got on the trail by 8:00 am. I pushed myself to rack up the miles as I was meeting a police officer from back home who was on spring break with his family and was planning on bringing me some dinner that night.

We planned to meet at Big Meadow Campground and I pushed hard to be there by 5 pm. Several miles before getting to the campsite, I came across a lady who was a day hiker near Skyline Drive. I said hello and before I knew it, we were chatting. When she found out I was a northbound thru-hiker, she offered me a beer. I followed her to her car that was parked in the parking lot and watched as she opened up the trunk of the car, only to discover that the cooler she thought was in the truck was not there but actually back at the campsite where she was staying. She apologized profusely for getting my hopes up. I laughed and told her it was no big deal and that I was meeting a friend for dinner anyway.

After getting to Big Meadow, I waited a few minutes until Jay and his family arrived. We sat at a picnic table and enjoyed a dinner of fries, a cheeseburger, and a piece of peanut butter pie. I ate it all in record time and washed it down with a soda. It really hit the spot and I thoroughly enjoyed getting to see some-one from back home. We talked about the trail and I thanked him for taking time out of his vacation to come and bring me food. I still had a good 4 miles to go in order to get to the shelter where I planned on staying, so I got back on the trail.

As I made my way on the trail that was skirting the edge of the campground, I saw something up ahead. At the base of a tree, there were two bottles of beer and a note. I picked up the note and read it. "To the thru-hiker we promised a beer to, please enjoy these at the shelter tonight." I smiled and placed both bottles in my pack and started pushing north again. I already had 20 miles in for the day and only had 4 more to do but I had a full belly and some beer to boot.

After making it to the shelter and doing all my nightly chores, I crawled into my quilt for the night. I had 14 miles to do the next day to get into Luray for a hostel stay. There were a few other section hikers staying at the campsite but I had the entire shelter to myself. It was a double-decker, so I positioned myself in the middle of the top deck hoping the resident mice would leave me alone. Looking out of the shelter, I could see the lights of Luray down in the valley. Being so close to town, I had decent cell service and I was able to call Laine and talk to her before drifting off to sleep. Life was good.

In the morning, I took my time leaving the shelter since I did not have a long day ahead of me. It was Friday and the weather reports were calling for possible snow on Saturday. My plan was to get into Luray and stay at Open Arms Hostel for the night. On Saturday, I planned on slackpacking 14.5 miles and getting picked up and taken back to the hostel. This would allow me to get some good miles in without having to sleep out in the weather and get some good food into my body.

I was able to get to the road crossing by early afternoon and was picked up by Allison, the hostel owner. When I got to the hostel, I took a nice hot shower and put on some loaner clothes while Allison washed my clothes. While I was there, Allison got a call and told me she would be picking up another hiker named Scratch. It was good to hear that Scratch would be spending the night and I told her I would wait until Scratch arrived to decide what to do about dinner. I stretched out on the bed and savored being clean and able to lay down on a real mattress. I called Laine and talked with her and then tried to catch up on what was going on in the world of social media. Above all, it was just nice to relax until it was time to eat again.

Eventually, Allison returned with Scratch. It was nice to see a familiar face and we decided to grab some dinner together after he got cleaned up and settled in. Earlier in the week, I was starting to feel a little discouraged when I found out that they were calling for more snow on the weekend. I had not planned out my next resupply and after all the snow I had already experienced, I was hoping for a break. Eventually, Laine was able to coordinate my stay at Open Arms. Having Laine at home to help coordinate hostels, shuttles, and other things was a huge burden that was lifted from me. She acted as my trail boss and was a huge part of my success as I navigated towards Maine.

When Scratch was ready, Allison drove us to an Italian restaurant not far from the hostel and told us to text her when we were done and she would come to get us. We both enjoyed our food and a beer and talked about trail life. Scratch was planning on hiking out the next morning and staying at a shelter that night. I told him about a place in Front Royal that was supposed to be pretty decent but he would have to put in a nearly 28-mile day. It would be a big day but he would have a warm place to stay. I, on the other hand, had decided to do half of it tomorrow and come back to Open Arms and then do the other half on

Sunday.

After finishing our meal, we text Allison and returned to the hostel. We both retreated to our rooms and got ready for bed. In the morning, Allison dropped us off at the trailhead and we headed into the woods. My plan was to stop for lunch at the Elk Hollow Wayside where I could buy a cheeseburger and fries. In Shenandoah National Park, there were places called "waysides" which were basically snack bars in the park. They are closed during the winter but I had gotten to the park just as most of them were opening up for the season. Since the terrain was fairly mild for the day and it was cold and they were predicting snow flurries, the thought of a big cheeseburger and fries motivated me to step it out and see how fast I could cover the 8.5 miles. I went ahead of Scratch as he slowed down to make a phone call and I told him I would probably see him at the wayside.

The easy terrain and the images of cheeseburgers in my head allowed me to cover those miles in 3 hours. I walked up to the wayside and left my pack outside by the door as I stepped inside. It was part camp store, part snack bar. I ordered a cheeseburger and fries with a Pepsi and got a hot pretzel to eat while I was waiting on my order. As they were cooking my food, in walked Scratch and he ordered some food also. They did not have any seating inside, only a bunch of picnic tables outside in the cold. While they were cooking Scratch's food, I quickly stood in the store and ate my food to avoid having to eat it in the cold outdoors.

After eating, we headed back on the trail, me to cover 6 more miles, and Scratch to head on to Front Royal. Once again, we wished each other good luck and parted ways. Before I knew it, I covered the 6 miles and got a ride back to the hostel. It was midafternoon and I showered and relaxed for the rest of the afternoon. Before dinner, another northbounder that I had passed on the trail a couple of days before arrived at the hostel. I wound up going to dinner with him and then to Walmart to resupply. I had one more day of hiking in Shenandoah National Park.

The next morning, it was sunny but pretty chilly. The temperatures only reached the mid-40s but I was able to stay warm as I hiked. I only had 13.5 miles to hike so I just tried to enjoy the day. At one point that morning, I came across an elderly couple who were visiting the park and were out on a day hike. They were stopped at a tree that had been clawed up by a bear. When I approached, they asked me about the tree and I explained to them that the tree damage was due to a bear looking for insects. We started to chat and I found out they were visiting the United States from Japan. Eventually, they asked me how far I was hiking. "Maine," I replied. I always enjoyed looking at the facial expressions when I told people that. Undoubtedly, the next question would be, "where did you start?" When I would reply with Georgia, their expressions would become even more enjoyable. I explained to them about the Appalachian Trail and what a thru-hike was. The husband asked if I would let his wife take a picture of he and I and I agreed. He then reached into his day pack and offered me two oranges. I accepted the oranges, slid them in the side pocket on my pack, and thanked him before setting off up the trail.

About an hour later, I stopped at a trail crossing at the top of a mild summit and found a log to sit on and enjoy some lunch. Since it was a Sunday, I encountered several day hikers and chatted with a few of them. After eating two spam tortillas, I pulled out the oranges I got from my Japanese trail angels and ate them before slipping my pack back on and hitting the trail northbound again. I was able to pull into Front Royal a little before 4:00 pm and got a place to stay at Mountain Home Cabbins, a small hostel run by a former thru-hiker and his wife. I ate a great dinner in town and was able to get some Dunkin Donuts coffee before heading back to the hostel. I was done with Shenandoah National Park and was sitting at mile marker 971.1 for the trip.

I was only two days away from hitting the 1,000-mile mark and three days away from Harpers Ferry, WV, the home of the Appalachian Trail Conservancy.

CHAPTER 11

Over The Hump

Even though I was almost through Virginia, the weather was still not showing signs of spring. When I left the hostel, the temperatures were in the 30s and there were snow flurries. The temperature did not warm up much throughout the day but at least the snow flurries did not turn into anything heavy.

The terrain wasn't too bad and I was trying to push a little over 23 miles for the day. Later in the afternoon, I approached a road crossing and saw something on the side of the trail just in from the road. As I got closer, I could tell it was a cooler and I picked up my pace. On top of the cooler was a note stating it was trail magic for thru-hikers from Cub Scout Pack 10 in Winchester. The best part was that it said, "Save one for the Scoutmaster." I opened up the cooler and saw an assortment of drinks and snacks. I grabbed a granola bar and a Dr Pepper and headed back on the trail.

I rolled into Red Hollow Shelter and got set up for the night. After eating dinner, I pulled out my trail guide and studied the terrain for the next day. I was sitting at mile marker 994.4. The next day, I would not only hit the 1,000-mile mark, but also enter the famous "Rollercoaster" and finally cross out of Virginia. The Rollercoaster is a stretch of trail that runs from just past Red Hollow Shelter north 13.5 miles. There are 10 climbs along the section, thus giving it the feeling that you are on a rollercoaster. The climbs are not long climbs but short and steep and once you get to the top of one, you immediately descend only to ascend again as soon as you hit the bottom.

I was able to talk to Laine earlier in the day and she had been communicating with a guy named Mike. Mike was an Assistant Scoutmaster from Boy Scout Troop 365 in Great Falls, VA and he was wanting to provide some trail magic for me and maybe slack-pack me. The plan was for Mike to meet me at a road crossing approximately 3 miles north of the shelter and he was going to allow me to leave some of my gear with him. He would then meet me at lunchtime to bring me lunch and then meet me later in the afternoon to bring my gear back to me.

I had the shelter all to myself that night and was able to sleep pretty well. I packed up that morning and headed back out onto the spur trail that took me back onto the AT and towards the Rollercoaster. I wasn't on the trail long before I came across a sign on a tree that announced my arrival at the Rollercoaster. I stopped to read the sign and then put my head down and started hiking. When I came to the first climb, I just kept my head down and pumped my legs up the mountain. It wasn't a long hike up but it was steep enough to break a sweat and get the heart pumping. As advertised, after reaching the summit, I started to descend at the same rate. When I reached the bottom, the trail arched upward again and took me even higher. As I climbed, I just thought about meeting Mike and getting to take a break and have a snack. After hiking down the second peak, I was just a 1/2 mile away from the road crossing where I was supposed to meet Mike.

I approached the road and saw him waiting in his car and I yelled out to him. He let me remove some stuff from my pack such as my tent, food bag, and a few other items and I placed them in his truck for safe keeping. He offered me a banana and I gladly accepted it and ate it as I stood there. He loaded me up with some drinks and snacks and we planned to meet me at Bear Den Rocks for lunch. I thanked Mike for helping me and hit the trail, pushing north towards the 1,000-mile mark.

As I hiked, I thought about all the milestones I was accomplishing on this day. So far, the worst thing about the Roller Coaster was that there were a decent amount of rocks on the trail and that was a little rough on the feet. The actual climbs were not that bad, as they were a little steep but usually not long. The weather was cool but there was no rain, so the only moisture was from my own sweat. As I hiked, I kept checking my location on Guthooks as I grew closer and closer to the 1,000-mile mark. There is a sign on a tree at the mile marker and I wanted to make sure I did not miss it as I wanted to get my picture at the sign.

Since the trail's mileage can change from year to year as trail maintenance crews are forced to re-route sections for various reasons, the sign is not at the current 1,000-mile mark but within a mile or so from it. When I passed the 1,000-mile mark on Guthooks, I was careful to check every tree that I passed looking for the iconic sign. Eventually, just as I was about to give up looking, thinking that I must have walked past it, I saw something up ahead on one of the trees. I pulled out my phone and started videoing my approach to the tree. As I got closer, I could see the simple wooden sign that read "1,000" in white numerals. There was nothing else on the sign. No words of congratulations, no fanfare, nothing. Just the simple four-digit number.

I took a picture of me standing in front of the sign and was able to text it to my wife and son. For the caption, I simply wrote "1,000 miles." After sending the text, I stood at the sign and just stared at it for a moment. I thought back to the cold days in Georgia and the snow as I hiked through Virginia. I thought about everything I had been through to that moment. I thought about the fact that I had just walked 1,000 miles. While

I still had nearly 1,200 miles to go, I could see that halfway point and soon I would no longer be counting up to Katahdin, but counting down.

Having nobody there with me to celebrate this huge accomplishment and knowing that Mike would be waiting for me with lunch, I did what I had been doing since Springer, I started pushing north again. While each day would bring new milestones and new mountains to climb and conquer, it was all just part of the deal. I had been on the trail for long enough to expect to accomplish these milestones. They were routine to me now. What most people would consider as amazing feats were just part of my daily routine. In short, I was a hiker, and hikers hike.

With 1,000 miles behind me and Mike waiting for me with Chick-Fil-A for lunch, I pushed as fast as I could to meet him. When I arrived at Bear Den Rocks, Mike was already there. We sat on the rocks on a beautiful outcropping and I devoured my lunch. We sat and talked for a bit after eating and Mike had me pose for a picture on the rocks. Again, he loaded me down with drinks and snacks and we agreed to meet at the trail crossing for the Blackburn Trail Center which was another 6 miles north.

Prior to getting to the final meeting point to meet Mike, I

crossed off another milestone on my list. I finally crossed out of Virginia and hit the West Virginia state line. I had completed four states and only had ten more to go. More importantly, I completed the longest state. It was such a huge mental relief to know that I was done with Virginia. Prior to hiking the trail, I had heard a lot about Virginia and what they call the "Virginia Blues." While I never really felt any sort of depression being in Virginia for so long, I did experience some very difficult times. Between the snow that I had to hike through and the loss of one of my scouts, my experience in Virginia was definitely one of tough times and heartbreak. Despite the tremendously difficult times in Virginia, I had survived. I made it through. I wasn't going anywhere but north to Maine.

As planned, I met up with Mike around 5 pm and got all my stuff back. He loaded me up with some food and more drinks. He also gave me one of his troop t-shirts. He definitely was a great trail angel and a true Scouter. While I enjoyed the experiences and the views on the trail, the best part of hiking the AT was definitely meeting people like Mike. Total strangers spending their time and money to help other total strangers. Knowing that I had people like Mike supporting me and cheering me on really helped keep me motivated to continue pushing north.

I hiked to the David Lessor Memorial Shelter and wound up sharing it with a young couple and their dog who were just starting a flip-flop hike of the AT. A flip-flopper was a hiker who, instead of starting at one end of the trail and hiking to the other continuously, they hike the entire trail by doing it in non-sequential sections.

Looking ahead to the next day, I was only about 8 miles from Harpers Ferry. I wasn't sure if I was going to stop and stay in Harpers Ferry or if I would just eat lunch there and visit the ATC Headquarters before hiking out. I was doing decent on food so I really did not need a resupply. I decided I would play it by ear and see how I felt after getting to Harpers Ferry. Harpers Ferry is known as the psychological half-way point for hikers because of the ATC Headquarters being located there, even though the actual halfway point is still approximately another 70 miles further north.

I left the shelter by 8:30 am and started the hike to Harpers Ferry. There was a decent amount of rocks on the trail but I was excited to get to the ATC, so I just kept pushing. I passed some day hikers on the way, including a couple of older gentlemen who were former thru-hikers. We stopped and chatted for a bit and they encouraged me by telling me stories of their climb up Mt. Katahdin. I thanked them for the words of encouragement and kept going. As usual, there was a descent into Harpers Ferry and a walk alongside the interstate before a short climb up into some woods, only to be dumped out onto the streets of Harpers Ferry.

It was a short walk to the ATC and when I arrived there, I pulled off my pack and set it and my hiking poles on the front porch. I walked into the building and was greeted by one of the employees. After letting her know I was a northbound thru-hiker, they grabbed their camera and led me back outside to the front porch to take my picture. It is tradition that thru-hikers get their picture taken when they arrive. The photograph is then placed in a scrapbook in order that the hiker arrived. They took my picture and informed me that I was the number 9 northbound thru-hiker for the year. There is a hiker lounge in the back of the room and they have free sodas for the thru-hikers. I got myself a Coke out of the refrigerator and sat down to look at the photo book and also to fill out a few picture postcards of me that I was going to mail home.

Looking at the photo book, I saw that Overhill and Fun Size were ahead of me, along with Scratch. It was good to see they were all still on the trail. I then walked around the building and checked out the displays they had to include a sign that used to be atop Mt. Katahdin. I asked one of the workers about good places to eat in town and was directed to an Italian place just a few blocks away. I walked down the street to the restaurant and had a calzone for lunch while I relaxed.

Since it was a nice day and it was still early, I decided not to stay in town and go ahead and hike about 7 miles to the Ed Garvey Shelter. Doing so would also put me in another state, Maryland. I headed out of Harpers Ferry and walked along the Potomac River for several miles before heading back up into the woods and arriving at the shelter. There were several section hikers there and I enjoyed chatting with them while I set up and cooked dinner. Tomorrow would be my first full day in Maryland and I was looking forward to being in Pennsylvania in two days.

It was raining on and off in the morning but it was supposed to clear up and be warm. I waited out the rain and hit the trail around 10 am. I was only planning to hike a little over 16 miles so I did not mind getting a late start. The trail was pretty easy except for a few rock pockets every now and then. In the afternoon, I made it to Washington Monument State Park and climbed up on top of the monument which is a large tower overlooking the area. At the top, I met an older gentleman and we struck up a conversation. While we were talking, I noticed a bald eagle circling overhead. I watched as the large bird glided against a clear blue sky.

I said goodbye to the gentleman and headed back down the tower and north on the trail. I got to the next shelter by 5:20 pm and was pleasantly surprised to not only have cell service but also good LTE service that allowed me to upload some videos. I had the shelter all to myself. While I enjoyed having other people around, it was nice to be alone and do my own thing. By this point in the trail, I actually looked forward to having the shelter and campsite all to myself. The temperatures got up to 70 degrees today and it felt great. Looking at the weather for the next day, the temperatures were going to continue to be warm. It was nice to finally get several warm days in a row.

I woke up and hit the trail in the morning knowing that I would be crossing into Pennsylvania and staying in a hotel that evening. I was able to push some good miles in the morning and had 12 miles logged by noon. As the afternoon sun heated up the day and more and more rocks started to appear, my pace slowed down some but I was still able to cross the Mason/Dixon Line bordering Maryland and Pennsylvania by 2:45 pm. I was now through 6 states and had 8 more to go.

I crossed the border and continued hiking towards Waynesboro, PA. Laine had reserved me a hotel in town that was situated right behind a Walmart and an all-you-can-eat Chinese buffet. I was really looking forward to getting a shower and washing some clothes. It was Friday and I was going to spend the night in a bed in a private hotel room. It could not get much better than that. As I was approaching the trailhead where I was supposed to meet my shuttle, I was hiking near a stream when a snake slithered off of a rock near me and disappeared into the stream. It was the first snake I had seen on the trail and it was a sign that spring was on its way.

After 20.6 miles for the day, I met the shuttle and got dropped off at the hotel. After a shower and some laundry, I headed to the Chinese buffet to satisfy my appetite. I ate four full plates of Chinese food and washed it all down with some Pepsi. The best part of hiking all those miles was the hiker hunger that you would get. I could eat anything I wanted and pretty much all I wanted and I would not gain weight, actually, I would lose weight. At times, I know people were probably thinking, "how can this little guy eat all that food?"

After eating, I resupplied at Walmart and got myself a foot-long sub at the Subway in Walmart that I could pack out for lunch the next day. As a quick dessert treat, I also got a hot pretzel and a Coke Icee to go. I was in a new state, my belly was full, and I was headed back to my hotel room for some nice rest and recovery. Life was good.

CHAPTER 12

Rocksylvania

Day 75 on the trail greeted me with a beautiful sunny day. After eating breakfast in the hotel room, I met my shuttle and got dropped back off at the trailhead. I planned an 18-mile day and had a warm but nice day to hike. The terrain was good and I only had to deal with rocks for about half the day. AT hikers affectionately refer to Pennsylvania as "Rocksylvania" due to the sheer amount of rocks that seem to pepper the trail. The southern part of the trail in the state is not too bad but the further north you travel in the state, the more rocks that appear.

I was able to stop and eat lunch at a beautiful lookout point and I made sure to take off my pack, have a seat, and pull out the Subway sandwich that I packed out from town. Since it was a Saturday and a beautiful day, there were plenty of day hikers out on the trail. After lunch, I was hiking while listening to some music through my earbuds when I came across a Boy Scout troop. They were from Maryland and were doing a two-day/one-night hike as a troop. I stopped and spoke with them. It was good to see a Boy Scout troop out hiking but it did make me miss my troop.

Since it was a warm day out, I was drinking more water than normal. There was a stretch where there was no water so I had to push a little farther to find some. Eventually, I came to a spur trail for a shelter that had a spring so I took the spur trail. The shelter was down 3/10s of a mile and the spring was 2/10s of a mile further. It was a pretty steep descent but I was completely out of water and needed to do what I could to get water. This was really the first time on the trail where I was literally out of water and needed some. I climbed all the way down to the spring and filtered myself over 2 liters of water in addition to drinking nearly another liter of water. While the hike down to the spring was not that bad, now I had to hike back up and do so with an additional 5 pounds of water in my pack. I could feel the extra weight but I was glad I had water.

Eventually, I crossed into Caledonia State Park and headed to the Quarry Gap Shelters. About a mile or so from the shelter, I ran into Jim, the innkeeper who maintains the shelter and the campsite. He asked me if I was heading to the shelter and told me there were a few other hikers there but there was still plenty of room. When I got there, I discovered two small shelters with a covered picnic area between them with a picnic table. In addition to that, a babbling brook ran right in front of the shelters and served as the water source. There were flowers planted around the campground and hanging plants. The privy was also pretty nice as it included toilet paper and had pictures hanging on the walls. Definitely the prettiest campsite I had stayed in.

The weather was going to take a turn for the worse over the next couple of days as they were predicting several inches of rain. As luck would have it, another subscriber to my YouTube channel contacted Laine and wanted to help me slack-pack for a few days. He wanted to pick me up in Pine Grove Furnace State Park, just past the official halfway point and take me into town to a hotel. I headed out under cloudy conditions but they were calling for rain and, eventually, the rain started. Fortunately, it was a light rain but they were calling for heavy rain in the late afternoon and throughout the evening.

The trail was mostly flat without many rocks, so I was able

to cover the 17 plus miles to the General Store in Pine Grove Furnace State Park in decent time. Along the way, I crossed the halfway point on the trail. I took a picture at the sign and kept on hiking. I had now come further on the trail than I had left to go. By the time I reached the General Store, I had also crossed the 1,100-mile mark. I was getting ever so close to having less than 1,000 miles left to hike. Arriving at the General Store, I saw a man sitting in a truck and he was speaking with another man. When he saw me approaching, he got out of his truck and greeted me. His name was Mike and he handed me a hot chocolate. Since it was a cool and rainy day, the hot chocolate was a nice treat. I loaded my backpack and poles in the back of the truck and climbed in the passenger's seat.

Mike was retired and originally from Texas. He was following my journey on YouTube and wanted to help. With the weather that was coming that evening and the next day, his help came at the perfect time. He drove me to Carlisle, PA and booked me into a hotel room for the next two nights. He paid for the rooms and then took me next door to a restaurant and told me I needed to order whatever I wanted. We sat and talked about the trail and discussed where some of the other hikers were and who was still on the trail. Since leaving Springer, I really did not keep up with all the other YouTubers. I had enough trouble getting my videos edited and uploaded, so I really did not have a chance to watch other videos.

Mike expressed his concern that he could really see a big difference in me regarding my weight since I started the trail. He was worried that I was losing weight too fast and needed to eat more so that I could have the energy to keep going on the trail. He wanted to slack-pack me for the next 2 days all the way to Duncannon. Along the way, I could eat a lot of town food and get some good rest in a hotel. This would allow me to cover almost 45 miles and with the rain that was coming that night and into the next day, I could dry out in the hotel.

After getting a good night's sleep, I woke up and got myself ready to meet Mike. He met me at the hotel and took me back to where I left off. It rained heavily all night long but had stopped. As luck would have it, as soon as Mike pulled away and I started to hike, the rain started again. With all the rain over the last 24 hours, the trail was saturated. Within minutes, both my feet had been completely submerged multiple times and it was obvious that wet feet were going to be the order of the day. The trail resembled a stream that I had to walk through as I sloshed my way north.

Several of the creek crossings no longer had exposed rocks that would normally allow you to rock hop across without getting your feet wet. They were all overflowing and the rocks were under 6-8 inches of water. Fortunately, the temperature outside was not bad, so I was able to keep my wet feet from freezing. After hiking in the rain for the first hour, the rain stopped and only returned as sprinkles on and off all day.

The trail was pretty flat and the few climbs were moderate which allowed me to keep a good pace. I reached Boiling Springs, PA and hiked through the town. The trail took me past the ATC office but I kept going as I wanted to make sure I was on time to meet Mike. Over the last few miles, I was able to maintain a 3-mile per hour pace with no problem and met Mike around 5 pm. My mileage for the day was 23.4 miles and I was headed back to the hotel to dry out and eat some good food.

Once again, Mike supplied me with some drinks and snacks and then dropped me off at the hotel for the night. I ordered a pizza and took a shower and started my laundry while I waited for my dinner to be delivered. Being able to put in big miles in wet conditions was a good accomplishment but being able to do that and get clean and dry at the end of the day was a huge mental lift. When all my clothes were washed and dried, I repacked my pack and prepared for the next day. I relaxed and enjoyed the simple comforts of the hotel room before getting into bed and drifting off to sleep.

In the morning, I met Mike in the lobby and headed with him back to the trail. My plan was to hike 21 miles to Duncannon and meet Mike for the last time to pick up some of my gear. The rain had finally moved out and it was a decent weather day to hike. In the morning, there was a decent amount of road walking and trekking through farmland. There were only two mountains to climb for the day and the first one was pretty easy. The second one was steep climbing up but ended up turning into a 4-mile ridge hike at the top that was nothing but rocks. It looked like someone had just dumped rocks of all shapes and sizes all over the ground. There was no way to walk around or in between the rocks. With each step, you were stepping on pointy, odd-shaped rocks. Rarely would your feet find a flat rock to step on and you had to be careful to balance yourself with each step.

Not only did the boulder fields slow you down because of the need to check your balance with each step, but they were brutal on your feet. With every step, the soles of my feet were being mashed by the rocks. My entire weight and the weight of my pack was forcing my feet into the rocks. After already hiking 1,100 plus miles, my feet were swollen and remained that way.

After navigating the 4-mile rock ridge, I started my descent into Duncannon. As I was moving further north into Pennsylvania, I was starting to hit more and more rocks. The descent into Duncannon was a great introduction for me to rocks and I had to be extra careful as a fall on the rocks going down could result in a hike-ending injury. I took my time and concentrated on each step. This only increased the mental fatigue and, coupled with the physical fatigue on my body, it made the minutes seem like hours.

Eventually, I made it into town and made my way to The Doyle Hotel, an old-time hotel that has an old-time bar/pub on the first floor and rooms on the top floors. The hotel is pretty run down but it is a common place for hikers to stop, eat, drink, and even stay. I arrived before Mike did and went inside and got a room for the night. After checking in, I made my way back outside and waited for Mike.

Soon, Mike arrived and I got all my stuff. As usual, Mike loaded me down with snacks and drinks and wished me a safe trip to Maine. Like a true trail angel, he sought no recognition and helped me when I needed it most. Once again, I was learning the lesson that the trail provides. Those trail angels who have never hiked the trail do not know how important their actions are to a thru-hiker. They truly are trail angels and they are part of what makes the AT a special place.

After saying goodbye, I made my way to the bar and met another hiker named Now or Never. He was hiking north but wasn't necessarily going all the way. We both ordered a cheeseburger, fries, and a beer and then sat together to enjoy our meal. He explained to me that he started hiking the previous year and then got off trail after hiking a few hundred miles. He started back where he left off this year and was going to hike until he did not want to hike anymore. He was retired and just trying to have a good time. After eating our burgers, we made plans to eat at Goodies across the street for breakfast in the morning. The place was highly recommended and even though we just ate a huge burger and fries, we were already planning our next meal.

Fortunately, it was not summertime as the rooms in the hotel had no air condition and I slept with the window open to make sure I did not get too hot during the night. I woke up and met Now or Never and we headed off to breakfast. I ordered some eggs and bacon and drank some coffee. It was great to have some eggs, as I did not get them very often on the trail. Most hostels serve pancakes or waffles if they serve a hot breakfast so it was nice to get some eggs. We chatted and ate our breakfast before heading back across the street to finish packing our gear and hitting the trail.

Now or Never headed out first as I needed to run by the Post Office to mail some winter gear home. The second half of Pennsylvania is where the rocks were going to increase in frequency. After hitting the Post Office and stopping in at a Subway to pack out a sub for lunch and dinner, I made my way out of Duncannon and towards the rocks. The weather was really nice and it looked to be a great day for a hike. After making the initial climb out of Duncannon, I hiked along a rocky ridge that took me through a series of boulder mazes. Despite the rocks, the hike was not that bad. I enjoyed half my sub sandwich for lunch and saved the rest for dinner.

About halfway through my 16-mile day, I caught up with Now or Never and we hiked together for the next 8 miles. We reached a small campsite and pitched our tents for the night. It was the first time in over two months that I slept in my tent but the next shelter was a good distance away so it was time to break it out. We were supposed to get some light showers overnight but they would stop before daylight.

As predicted, it did rain some but it stopped prior to daylight. I got packed up before Now or Never and wished him luck before heading north. I did not expect to see him again as I was planning on pushing about 18 miles to a campsite. It was my 80th day on the trail and I was getting closer and closer to Delaware Water Gap and seeing Laine again. About an hour into the hike, I met another NOBO named Walkie Talkie. He came up from behind me and we started hiking together. When I asked him where his trail name came from, he explained, "when I walk, I talk." As we hiked, we talked about what we did for a living and anything else we could think of to talk about. He was planning on hiking to the William Penn Shelter but I was planning to go to a campsite 8 miles before the shelter.

Time seemed to fly as we were hiking, despite some on and off showers that we hiked through. Before I knew it, it was 12:30 pm and I had covered nearly 12 miles. At that point, I decided that I would push through and head to the shelter with Walkie Talkie. Not only would it allow me to stay in a shelter and not a tent, but it would also be my biggest day to date on the trail, 26.4 miles. We hiked and talked and, eventually, in the afternoon, we came across some trail magic with my name on it. It was a cooler filled with Mountain Dews, pastries, and several other snacks. I offered some to Walkie Talkie and we both took a break, ate and drank. While we were standing there feeding our faces, two section hikers came by and we offered some magic to them. It was just what we needed to carry us through the rest of the day.

At 6:15 pm we saw the sign for the shelter and walked into the campsite and got set up. The temperatures were starting to drop and neither of us were wanting to cook. We sat on the edge of the shelter and rummaged through our bags for food we didn't have to cook. Walkie Talkie had an extra protein bar and offered it to me. I accepted it and ate it as I tried to stay warm. After dinner, we both retreated to the loft of the shelter and crawled into our bags and laid down for a much-deserved long winter's nap.

In the morning, Walkie Talkie headed out before me as he was meeting his ride to take him to a wedding he needed to attend. For me, Laine had arranged with a local Scouter for me to hike to Hawk Mountain Scout Reservation and spend the night camping with some scout people. I had to hike about 13.5 miles and it was pretty rocky. It wasn't that there were big rocks, there were tons of small pointy rocks that covered the entire ground and trail. It was brutal on my feet but I continued to press on. Eventually, I came to the road crossing where I was set to meet the Scouters.

Within minutes, I was being picked up and taken to meet my hosts for the evening. After arriving at camp and meeting Brian, my host, I took a nice hot shower. I ate dinner with Brian and several others and then retired to a cabin that they provided for me. I was sitting at mile marker 1,200 and had just under 1,000 miles to go to reach Katahdin. It was such a good feeling to see the remaining miles to hike number dip below four digits. Better yet, in five days, I would get to see Laine again. Every mile I hiked and every day that went by, I was getting closer and closer to seeing her.

Waking up early, I joined my fellow Scouters for breakfast and thanked them for their hospitality. I was driven back to the trailhead and continued the journey towards Maine. It was a sunny day and as the day went on, the temperatures warmed up. There was a decent amount of rocks on the trail but I was still able to make some good time. My plan was to hike into Port Clinton which was only 14.5 miles and I was able to get there by 3 pm. I made my way to the Port Clinton Hotel and booked myself a room. After getting some laundry going and taking a shower, I got ready to meet some friends of mine for dinner.

Around 5 pm, I was picked up by my friend, Corey, and his wife, Jessica, and daughter, Ryleigh. They lived in Pennsylvania and had been following my hike since the beginning. Ten months earlier, I met them for breakfast when I had flown up to be with my brother in his final hours. It was during that breakfast that I told them I was going to hike the trail. We discussed all that was involved in hiking the trail and made plans then for us to get together when I came through the area. It was a good feeling to see them and think about that conversation we had 10 months earlier. I had come a long way since then.

We went to dinner at a steakhouse and then hit a Walmart and Wawa for me to resupply. It would be the last town stop for me before I met up with Laine. I had 77 miles to cover in four days and some of Pennsylvania's rockiest terrain was waiting for me. After a good evening with friends, I returned to the hotel and went to bed. In the morning, I packed my gear into my backpack and headed back out on the trail.

The air was cold and crisp but they were calling for the temperatures to climb into the 60s by the afternoon. The sun was out and it looked to be a nice day for a hike. I was able to knock off 10 miles by lunchtime and found a nice rock to sit on and eat my lunch. I dug through my food bag and pulled out a couple of tortillas and found a pack of pepperoni that I had been carrying around for a good week or so. I was tired of looking at it so I made myself a pepperoni burrito and ate it before pushing on north.

About an hour and a half after lunch, I could feel my stomach starting to cramp and I was getting nauseous. As bad as it was to think about, I was hoping the reason for my discomfort was more food poisoning rather than the alternative. The alternative was Norovirus or Giardia, both ailments that would affect me for a lot more than a day or so. As I hiked, I prayed that I would feel better, but the further I went, the more obvious it seemed that I definitely was going to get sick. As I dug my hiking poles in the ground in front of me, I pushed myself along, using whatever strength I had in my arms and shoulders.

Finally, I could feel the inevitable and I leaned over the side of the trail and lost whatever nutrition I had eaten for lunch that day. After a few moments, I regained my composure and kept pushing forward. I had to stop and repeat my actions again before I came across a shelter spot. I was able to use the privy but when I was finished, I had a decision to make. I was at a shelter that was alongside a road and I was trying to decide if I needed to try to go into the nearest town and see a doctor. I still had several miles I wanted to cover that day and, of course, I kept thinking about the miles I needed to cover in order to meet Laine in three days.

I decided to push on and try to make it to the next shelter which was 7.4 miles ahead. After going about a mile and having to stop several times to vomit, I started to second guess my decision to keep going. I was beginning to make a climb and I looked at Guthooks to see if there were any tent sites before the shelter. Sure enough, there was a tent site approximately 1.5 miles north at the top of the climb I was doing. I wasn't able to hike fast but I hiked the best that I could. I would walk for about 50 feet and have to stop for a few minutes as I fought back the sickness and the cramping.

Finally, I reached a small campsite at the top of the summit I was climbing and immediately set up my tent. I had not used the tent for quite some time but I was happy to get it set up and lay down inside it. A couple of times I had to roll on my stomach and stick my head out of the door to vomit, but after, I would lay on my back and stare at the ceiling of my tent. I remained in that position for two hours until the sun was getting ready to go down. Eventually, I mustered whatever strength I had and got up and finished setting up camp for the night. I was in no mood to do any eating and probably could not keep anything down if I tried.

I reached into my food bag and was able to retrieve some flavored electrolyte drink mix and made myself a liter of electrolytes. Finally, around 9 pm that evening, I was able to slowly sip some electrolytes and try to re-hydrate my body which was clearly in need of some fluids. Eventually, I was able to fall asleep and get some much-needed rest. As the evening went on, I started to feel better. When I woke up the next morning, I went to the bathroom and tried to eat part of a honey bun. My stomach felt ok but I could tell I was dehydrated and my energy levels were pretty low.

I packed up my tent and gear and headed back onto the trail. It was Monday morning and Laine was set to meet me on Wednesday afternoon at the Delaware Water Gap. Since I had to cut my day short because I was sick, I now needed to cover almost 60 miles in the next three days. Fortunately, the weather looked good for the next two days so I decided to see how far I could make it. I knew it would take some time for me to get my strength back, so I decided to take it easy and try to drink as much as I could. Fortunately, I still had some electrolyte mix so I just drank it and slowly introduced food back into my system. I didn't feel sick anymore but felt worn out and had no energy.

Not long after getting back on the trail, I heard someone hiking up the trail behind me. I stopped and turned to see Scratch coming up the trail. It was a pleasant surprise to see a familiar face. We started to hike together and caught each other up with our trip since we last saw each other. I followed behind Scratch for a while until it became clear that I did not have the energy to keep up. I continued hiking and watched as Scratch slowly got further and further ahead until, eventually, he disappeared into the woods. I was alone again but I didn't mind as I was starting to enjoy just hiking by myself.

I made it to the Allentown Shelter and stopped to take a break and use the privy. I ran into some section hikers there and chatted a bit with them. After filtering some water and trying to eat a little bit, I got back on the trail. As the day went on and I started to drink more and more, I began to feel much better. Eventually, I was able to reach the Oven Bake Shelter and stop there for the night. After all was said and done, I was able to hike 15 miles. Not bad considering I was recovering from food poisoning. I was able to eat my normal dinner that night and really loaded up on some water and electrolytes.

I spoke to Laine and found out she was contacted by a YouTube subscriber who wanted to meet me the next day and slack-pack me. His name was Dale and he was going to meet me 2.5 miles north of the shelter and then slack-pack me 16 miles. I was scheduled to hike the Superfund site in Palmerton, which was a huge rock scramble. Between that and the fact I was getting over being sick, the trail had provided me another opportunity when I needed it most. I crawled into my quilt and went to sleep in order to rest up for the big day I had planned for tomorrow.

I woke up and packed up, getting on the trail by 7:45 am to meet Dale. I got to the road crossing and waited for Dale to arrive. After a few minutes, he pulled up and got out to greet me. I unloaded most of the stuff in my pack and put it in Dale's truck. He opened a cooler and provided me with some Gatorades and the biggest sub sandwich I had ever seen in my life. Having grown up in New Jersey, I had seen some big sub sandwiches before, but never one this big. It was well over a foot-long and had to weigh several pounds all by itself. It was a good thing I was slackpacking because this thing never would have fit into my backpack.

Dale agreed to meet me almost 18 miles up the trail at a gap where he would bring my gear for me to pick up before hiking a few more miles to a shelter. I threw on my pack and headed out. The weather was beautiful and I was feeling pretty good after drinking one of the Gatorades Dale had given me. As I hiked, I got closer and closer to Palmerton. After crossing the highway, I began the nearly 900-foot climb that spanned 1 mile. The top half of Blue Mountain was completely void of any vegetation due to a zinc smelting plant nearby that killed all the vegetation. The area has been a Superfund site since the early 1980s and a water source on the top of the mountain was only supposed to be used in an emergency due to heavy metal content in the water.

As I climbed, the trail was nothing more than large boulders with white blazes painted on them. Even though it was a steep climb, it was actually pretty fun. There were some parts where you had to hug the rocks and carefully plan out your next step, making sure you had a good foot hold before moving on. While climbing, I made a conscious effort not to turn around and look down as heights were really not my thing. I was grateful that I had a nice sunny day to climb as it would have been really sketchy to have to climb the rocks if they were wet. Before too long, I reached the top of the climb and headed north a bit on the trail before finding a good location to eat some lunch.

I took off my pack and had a seat on a rock overlooking Palmerton. Pulling the sub sandwich out of my pack, I had to laugh at the size of it. I was able to eat half of it while enjoying the beautiful weather and views the trail had provided for me. I drank some electrolytes and could feel that my body seemed to be fully recovered from the food poisoning. I was able to post a few pictures on social media and get a phone call out to Laine before getting back on my feet and hiking along the ridge for a while. By 4:15 pm, I reached Smith Gap Road and texted Dale to come and meet me. While I waited, I ate the other half of my Roast Beef sub and it wasn't long before Dale pulled up. He topped off all my water and hooked me up with some more Gatorade before giving me my stuff back and chatting while I re-packed everything into my pack.

I thanked Dale for all the help and told him he did not know how important it was for me to get this trail magic when I did. As I headed back into the woods, I had 3.5 more miles to go to get to the shelter I planned on staying at for the night. I thought about how 48 hours earlier, I was on all fours puking my guts out and now I was on my way to a 23.5-mile day and within 24 hours, I would be with Laine. Other than some rocks in the trail, the route to the shelter was pretty flat.

When I arrived at the shelter, I was the only one there and I quickly set up camp and made dinner. My appetite had re-turned. I was eventually joined by a southbound section hiker and another couple that was hiking. We were supposed to get rain overnight and on and off rain all day the next day. At that point, I really did not care as only 21.1 miles separated me from Laine.

By the time I headed out the next morning, the rain had let up. The trail was very rocky and I found myself constantly looking down to make sure I was placing my feet in the correct spots. There were times where I started to think to myself, "what does it feel like to feel dirt under my feet?" It was as if someone had dumped millions of rocks all over the ground. It wasn't just the trail that had rocks, at times, the surrounding area just looked like a massive field of sharp pointy rocks. Despite the rain and the rocks, I was actually maintaining a pretty good pace.

Eventually, I came to Wolf Rocks and came across a cooler of trail magic that had my name on it. YouTube subscribers, Chris and Shannon, had left it there and I gladly took a break and enjoyed a Gatorade before getting back on the trail. I ate lunch as I hiked and then got a text from Laine saying that she was at Delaware Water Gap and had checked into the hotel. As I hiked, I caught myself constantly checking my watch and hoping that the time would go by faster so that I could see Laine.

When I reached the top to Mt. Minsi, I could see the Delaware River and Rt 80 below. It started to rain again but I did not care. I tried to hike as fast as I could down the mountain, making sure of my footing so that I would not fall. At the bottom of the mountain, I walked through the town of Delaware Water Gap and headed towards Rt. 80 and the Delaware River. When I reached Rt. 80, I followed the trail as it took me across the Delaware on a pedestrian walkway as the trucks and cars flew past me and the rain steadily came down on me.

I knew on the other side of the river was Laine waiting for me. As I crossed above the river, I looked over to my right to the banks of the river and thought back to fishing from that bank with my brother when I was 18 years old. I also thought about all the times my family and I had driven across this very bridge as we were headed to the Poconos. As I got halfway across, I could see the paint on the concrete walkway that marked the state line of Pennsylvania and New Jersey. When I crossed the line into my eighth state, I realized that I had officially walked home. For the first time on the trail, I knew exactly where I was and it was an incredible feeling to know that I walked there.

I neared the end of the bridge and the trail headed down into a parking area where I saw my wife holding an umbrella walking towards me. I picked up the pace and when I reached her, I gave her a kiss. We retreated to the car and I threw my pack and poles in the back and climbed into the passenger's seat. Waiting for me in the cup holder was a hot cup of Dunkin Donuts coffee. Rocksylvania was done, I was with Laine, and all was good on the trail.

CHAPTER 13

Making Miles

There is no feeling as good as getting to see family when you are on the trail. After hiking nearly 600 miles, I was again reunited with Laine. At times, it seemed like a long time since I had seen her but then it seemed like it was just yesterday since she dropped me off at Catawba and I was hiking up to McAfee Knob. It was Wednesday afternoon and she was going to be with me until Sunday morning. I planned on slackpacking Thursday and Friday before taking a zero-day on Saturday and getting back on the trail on Sunday.

As a child, I spent every summer here in the Poconos, and getting to be here for a few days felt good. After taking a shower and changing into some real clothes that Laine brought for me to wear, we met my sister-in-law, niece, and her fiancé for dinner. I only wished my brother would have lived long enough to be there too. I think he would have enjoyed getting to see me while I hiked the trail. It was nice to get to see family and I had planned to see as much of my family as I could while I was in the area.

On Thursday morning, Laine dropped me off back near the bridge and I headed out with a lightened pack as I was planning on covering 16.7 miles hopefully by 3 pm. It was a beautiful day and the trail was pretty decent. There were a few ups but nothing too bad. I hiked and tried to get some pictures and just take in the scenery. At some point during the day, I was expected to pass above Boy Scout Camp NoBeBoSco. It was the summer camp that my Scout troop had been attending for the last several years. Each time we went to camp, I would hike up to the ridge behind the lake and connect to the AT. Just 9 months earlier, I hiked up to the AT from the camp and thought about what it would be like to hike on that trail having traveled all the way from Georgia.

It was sometime after lunch when I emerged from the woods and entered a field. From past experience, I knew that field was situated right above some power lines that were in the camp parking lot. I kept moving forward and followed the trail to a rock outcropping that provided an unobstructed view to the camp down below. As I approached the rock outcropping, I saw something on one of the trees. When I got closer, I could tell it was a wooden sign that was tied to the tree. "Welcome to NoBe Glenn" the sign read. An arrow pointed north to Katahdin and another pointed south to Springer.

Some of the camp staff had made the sign for me and tied it to the tree to welcome me to the area. I untied the sign and placed it in my backpack as a keepsake. While every bit of trail magic was special and appreciated, seeing this welcome sign warmed my heart. Having people that I actually knew leave something to welcome and inspire me really felt good. With a renewed sense of excitement, I pushed north, traveling the last few miles before coming to a parking area where Laine was waiting for me. It was 3:25 pm and my day was complete.

On Friday, I was dropped off again and hiked another 16.3 miles in on and off rain before meeting Laine and heading to my hometown of East Rutherford, NJ to spend the night. We spent a great night in my hometown having dinner and driving around, seeing all the places where I grew up. On Saturday, we had plans to visit with my brother for breakfast, a few cousins for lunch and more cousins for dinner during my zero-day. As Saturday night arrived, we spent time at C&J's, which is a special place owned by my cousins, Steve and Sue. They live in a log cabin in the Poconos and converted their basement into the ultimate man-cave. It is a full-fledged bar complete with an old-time jukebox, pinball machine, and even a stage. It is named after both their Dads, Charlie and Joe, and as the saying goes, it's "Always a good time at C&J's!"

Later in the evening, we went back to the hotel, where I would spend my last night with Laine. The next morning, I would be dropped off by Laine for the last time on this trip. While that was an exciting thing to think about, it was also sad. Having to say goodbye was always difficult, much more difficult than climbing mountains.

By the time I ate breakfast, packed everything up, and arrived at the trailhead, it was 10 am. My plan was to try to go nearly 23 miles, so with the late start, I would be pressed to get to my shelter spot for the night before darkness fell on the trail. It was in the 40s and cloudy which seemed to match my mindset and mood. It was so hard to leave Laine but I kept reminding myself that the next time I saw her, I would be a thru-hiker and we wouldn't have to say goodbye again. We hugged, kissed, and said goodbye. I grabbed my trekking poles and dug them into the ground as I pushed my body forward and northward.

Most people think about the physical part of hiking the trail when they contemplate doing a thru-hike. They focus on making sure they have all the correct gear and some luxuries from home that they believe will make their trek more enjoyable. While those considerations are important, the mental aspect is the one aspect that I believe is most important. Your body will adapt to the physical requirements of the trail and, over the years, many have hiked the trail with heavy or sub-standard gear by today's standards. The one thing that does not change is the mental toughness that is needed to do the entire trail.

Whether you hike the trail alone or with others, you inevitably will be alone with your thoughts a lot. In order to survive the entire trail, you must be able to be mentally tough. Leaving home and loved ones is very difficult. It becomes even more difficult when you must do so multiple times throughout the hike. Even stopping in a town for the night, while it is a nice break from the trail, the mental fortitude to leave the comfort of the town and get back on the trail is invaluable. It was usually easier if the weather was nice but when it wasn't, it made it that much harder.

The more times I saw Laine and then had to leave her did not make it any easier to do. I would try to distract myself with music or other types of thoughts so that I did not dwell on the immense sadness leaving her again would bring. For now, it was the thought that I was now embarking on the last section before seeing her for good. All I needed to do was hike and get back in the groove. As soon as I did that, my mind would get right and I would be back in the groove.

The first part of the trail had some rocks but they subsided after a while and I was able to make some good time. As the day wore on, I was focused on just getting to the shelter. By 7:10 pm, I was able to walk into the shelter site. It was tough leaving Laine but the best way to deal with the separation was just getting back in the rhythm. By the time I got to the shelter and started my nightly routine, the sadness of leaving Laine started to subside. I was all by myself, so I immediately got set up and cooked some dinner and ate. Having hiked 23 miles in 9.25 hours, I was tired and looking forward to getting some sleep. I was 90 days into my trek and was sitting at mile marker 1351.5 miles. The next day, I would walk out of New Jersey and into New York, my ninth state on the journey.

The air was cold when I woke up and I had to force myself to get out of my warm quilt and get going. The temperatures were only going to reach the 40s and it was forecasted to rain on and off all day. I was planning a 23.6-mile day. It was 7:30 when I got on the trail and I was greeted with more rocks. Fortunately, I was able to hike for three hours before any rain came but it was still slow going. I found myself racing against the clock to get to the shelter before nightfall. As I was hiking over some rocks, I looked down and saw some white paint on the rocks that denoted I was about to cross out of New Jersey and into New York. Another state down and another state closer to Maine.

The last couple of miles before the shelter were relatively easy and rock-free. I was finally able to get a good pace going and rolled into the shelter at 7:15 pm. There were two other hikers at the shelter when I got there, a section hiker from Manhattan and another NOBO named Maple. I had seen his name in a few shelter journals in NJ and had finally caught up with him. He was an 18-year-old guy from Vermont and was nursing an injury. I quickly made dinner and was able to eat and clean up before it got dark. We all got settled and laid down to get some sleep.

When morning arrived, I packed up and prepared for more rocky climbs. The section hiker who stayed at the shelter was familiar with the trail I was about to encounter and he told me it was a bunch of short steep climbs that were all rock scrambles. Some even had rebar in the rock so you would have a foothold to place your feet. As I hiked that day, I realized that he was absolutely correct. Every rock climb I would encounter would generate a sense of irritation from me. In all the research I had done prior to starting my hike, nobody ever mentioned how tough New York state was going to be. I expected the rocks in Pennsylvania and even expected some rocks starting out in New Jersey, but I did not expect the rocky climbs in New York. It sort of made me angry, but I just focused on getting it done. My pace was less than 2 miles an hour, which frustrated me. Eventually, the last 6 or 7 miles before the shelter, the trail got less rocky and I was able to pick up the pace. Again, I rolled into the shelter after 7 pm and was glad to be there. The weather did warm up considerably which was nice. The next couple of days were going to be really warm, in the 80s, and I was looking forward to being warm for once.

Laine had been contacted by a New York City Fireman named Mike who wanted to help me out and offered to meet me to take me to resupply. We arranged to meet the next day in the morning right on the Palisades Parkway at the visitor's center. I woke up and hit the trail by 7:15 am so that I could meet him and get some breakfast. After climbing Black Mountain and getting a view of New York City, I descended the mountain and made it to the meet-up location with Mike. He was waiting for me and we drove to the nearest town and went to IHOP. At IHOP, I ordered a big breakfast and some hot coffee. Mike and I sat and talked. It was nice to relax and just have a good breakfast. Mike treated me to breakfast and then took me to Walmart to resupply.

Walmart is known on the trail as the premier place to re-supply. It not only has everything a thru-hiker could want or need, but it has the best variety of food at cheap prices. I went through the aisles and grabbed my share of food to get me to the next stop. On my way out of the store, I saw they had a Subway and I stopped in to get me a sub to pack out for lunch. Mike drove me back to the visitor's center and I thanked him for all the help. Getting resupplied was going to allow me to stay on the trail for longer before having to go back into town and the breakfast and lunch I was packing was going to give me some much-needed calories.

As expected, I had a big climb right at the onset. It was getting really warm out but I did not care. After all the cold and snow I had endured earlier on the trail, the warmth was a nice change of pace. I made it up the mountain only to climb back down as I had done for hundreds of miles. I was now facing Bear Mountain and I started to make the 700-foot climb up the mountain. About halfway up, there were some ledges that provided a beautiful view to West Mountain. It was time to take a break and pull out that Subway sub I had packed out of town.

Along with a soda I packed out, I took off my pack, kicked off my shoes, and sat down for lunch. It was a beautiful sunny day, the type of day that everyone thinks of when they think of hiking the AT. I had good food, a good view, and nothing but time to enjoy it.

After a nice long lunch break, I shouldered my pack and continued up Bear Mountain. At the top, there is an observation tower but there were also a bunch of tourists. I started to make my way down the mountain and ran into dozens upon dozens of tourists as there is a resort on the mountain. Finding a vending machine, I bought a Snapple Iced Tea and gulped it down. It was hot outside and I was trying to drink as much as I could. I continued on and came across the Trailside Zoo and Museum. The AT actually goes right through the zoo and then dumps you out on the Bear Mountain Bridge. The Bear Mountain Bridge crosses the Hudson River and is the lowest elevation on the entire AT at 180 feet.

As I crossed the bridge, the trail started to climb in elevation. It was only about a 700-foot climb but it was pretty steep. Combined with the heat, I was sweating like a pig and my clothes were drenched. After making the climb, the trail settled down some and was not too bad. I was planning on staying at the Graymoor Spiritual Life Center which was a pavilion at a baseball field where hikers were allowed to camp. Less than a mile from the side trail to the pavilion, I came across the Appalachian Market. It was a 24-hour deli, a grill, and had anything a hiker could want and I was wanting a cold drink. I took off my pack and propped it up outside against the building and walked inside. It was 5 pm and the first thing I saw when I walked in was the counter and a menu of all the stuff they offered. Since I was not far from where I was going to be camping for the night and it was only 5 pm, I decided to order me the biggest bacon cheeseburger they had and a large order of fries and a drink.

I sat down at one of the small tables and waited as they

cooked my food. It had been a hot day but it was a great day for eating as I was able to eat IHOP, Subway, and now a big bacon cheeseburger and fries. After a few minutes, my food was ready and I dug in. Nothing tastes better than a big bacon cheeseburger and fries when you have put in a long, hot day of hiking. I stuffed the last few fries into my mouth before getting up and heading back outside to retrieve my pack. As I headed to Graymoor, I was moving a little slowly with all that food in me, but it felt good. When I arrived at the pavilion, there were two section hikers already there. As it turned out, they were both scout leaders so after setting up to sleep on one of the picnic tables in the pavilion, we spent an hour or so talking and hanging out. As the sun went down, I got into my quilt and relaxed. I was past 1,400 miles and, all in all, had a pretty good day.

The next day was another hot one and I drank over 7 liters of water and still could not stay hydrated. I ran into Maple and we hiked a good part of the day together until later in the afternoon when I stopped for a break and he continued on. As I neared mile 20 for the day, I was approaching the RPH Shelter and had to speed up to beat a late afternoon shower that was about to fall. As the initial drops started to fall, I gained on the shelter until, finally, I arrived and ducked inside. The shelter looked like an old garage that had a covered picnic area in front and two wooden bunk beds inside. I was close to a road and right behind someone's backyard. Maple was already there and I made myself at home.

I was laying down in my quilt and Maple was outside on the phone when a hiker came out of the darkness and walked into the shelter. His name was Freak Out and he was a NOBO from Belgium. Even though it was already dark, he was debating whether or not he was going to stay or push on to the next shelter. As I would later learn, Freak Out was hiking big miles and it wasn't unusual for him to hike late into the night or push 30-40 miles straight. Eventually, he decided to stay and we all settled down for the night.

In the morning, we all sat around the picnic table and ate breakfast together. Freak Out had never been in America before and we talked about some of the people and things he had experienced since being on the trail. We were a couple of days away from Pauling, NY and he was contemplating picking up the train in Pauling and going into New York City for a zero. He had a friend that lived in the city and he had never been there. I told him he should do it since he was so close. After eating, we all packed up our gear and headed out. Maple left first and then I headed out with Freak Out not far behind. The weather was calling for some rain and, eventually, we did get a little bit. I could tell that my energy stores were a little low so I tried to take it easy. I initially thought about doing 18.9 miles to town and getting a place to stay but I was concerned that with the low energy and decent number of miles, I would get to town late and then not get all my chores done before it was time for bed.

In the end, I decided to hike 15.8 to a shelter and then hike the next 3.1 the following day and take a Nero day in town. I had been going pretty hard since leaving Laine and with the two hot days I had just done this week, my energy stores were pretty much tapped out. Having a Nero day in town would allow me to food up and rest up as I was almost out of New York and was about to enter into New England. I was able to get to the shelter by 4:30 pm and met a husband and wife section hiker couple. They were from New York City and the husband was a lawyer. Being a lawyer myself, we exchanged lawyer stories and had a good time. They even shared some chicken and dumplings with me. I was really looking forward to a light day the next day and could not wait to eat some good food in town.

After eating some breakfast and packing up the next morning, I got on the trail for a nice leisurely hike to the road crossing that would lead me into town. It was a beautiful day and I was looking forward to some good food and relaxation. As I hiked, I heard some crashing in the woods to my right. I turned my head to the right just in time to see a black bear lumbering up the mountain away from me. He apparently heard or saw me coming and was trying to get out of there. When I got less than half a mile from Rt 22, I came across the Swamp River Boardwalk. On the boardwalk, there was some trail magic left and I found a bag of pretzels and grabbed them and started to eat some as I headed towards the road crossing where I would go into town.

When I reached the road, I turned left and walked beside the road and came to a Landscaping place that had drinks for sale. I stopped in for a cold drink and spent 15-20 minutes chatting with the lady who was manning the register. After speaking for a while, I continued on to the town of Wingdale. It was a several-mile road walk but since it was a beautiful day and it was only 10:30 in the morning, I decided to walk it. On the way to the hotel, I stopped in at a pizza place and got myself a large pepperoni pizza and ate the entire thing. I washed it all down with a 2-liter bottle of Nestea Iced Tea. My hiker hunger had definitely set in. After eating and checking into a hotel, I spent the rest of the day washing clothes, eating, and relaxing. Tomorrow, I would walk out of New York and I couldn't be happier. I was ready to enter the last section of the AT, New England.

CHAPTER 14

Spring Arrives

My last day in New York greeted me with some light rain, just like my first day in New York did. I was set to enter into Connecticut and I was pretty excited with the thought that I was going to be in New England. The only worry I had was the conditions of the mountains in Vermont, New Hampshire, and Maine. A few days earlier, I heard that Overhill made it to Vermont but hit some pretty heavy snowfall. As a result, after finding himself hiking in waist-deep snow, he decided he had had enough and went home to California. The realization that a young guy like him, someone who had already hiked the Pacific Crest Trail, could wind up not completing the AT was a stark reminder that as far as I had traveled, there was a lot more to do. Overhill was averaging well over 22 miles a day, but it seemed that despite the miles he was making, he got to New England too early. Spring had not arrived in New England yet and the remnants of winter had claimed a casualty.

I wondered if I had started the trail too early. I was hoping that there would be enough time for the snow to melt before I got to Vermont. Vermont would be the first time I would climb a 4,000-footer since Southern Virginia and after seeing a picture of the snow that Overhill faced, I prayed things would warm up and give that snow a chance to melt. Before lunchtime, the rain had stopped and I crossed into Connecticut. As I hiked, I ran into a couple of hikers, one of whom was a former thru-hiker and they were out on a section hike headed southbound. I stopped and chatted with them and the topic of my start date came up. They were shocked to see me this far north so early and I told them I hoped I didn't start too soon. The thru-hiker could sense my uncertainty on whether I would hit some snow issues in Vermont, New Hampshire, and Maine but he quickly reassured me I would be fine. I reiterated my concern on the snow issue and he again looked at me and told me in no uncertain terms that I would be fine.

I don't know what it was, but that was just the type of encouragement I needed to stop worrying about the snow and keep pushing north. As the weather cleared up some, I was able to speak with Laine and find out that a subscriber had left some trail magic for me at the shelter I was planning on staying at for the night. When I arrived at the shelter, there were three section hikers already there and they told me about the trail magic that was waiting for me. There were sodas, pastries, candy bars, and more. In addition, someone had left several cans of beer at the shelter. Definitely more than I could eat by myself and, fortunately, a few minutes after arriving, Freak Out showed up and I shared some with him. He was planning to hike on but did stop long enough to have a snack, drink and chat with us. It was an 18-mile day for me but I had a great night chatting with the section hikers before laying down to get some sleep.

The next day was beautiful. The sun was shining and the temperature got up to 70 degrees. As I hiked, I pulled out my phone to take a video and I noticed something as I looked through the camera. The forest was green. For the first time on the trail, it seemed like the entire landscape was green and bright. I thought to myself, spring has finally arrived. Here I was in Connecticut and, finally, I had walked long enough to feel like spring had arrived. The scenery was beautiful and it brightened my mood. I don't know if it was just because everything was green but Connecticut had become my favorite state so far.

That afternoon, I was about to start a climb when I got a text message from Laine asking me to call her when I got a chance. I was able to get a call out and got her on the phone. She told me she got a call from the local scout council informing her that Cotter's Eagle Scout credentials were received from the National Office and he was officially an Eagle Scout. While the news was not unexpected, it was definitely welcomed. It was still early in the afternoon and I knew Cotter's Mom would still be at work, so I decided to continue climbing and get to the summit before trying to call her.

When I reached the top of the mountain, I was able to check my phone for service and, sure enough, I not only had several bars of service but also had some LTE service. I dialed the phone and stared out across the valley below as I waited until she answered. Obviously, she was surprised to hear from me out on the trail but I told her I had some news for her. Not wanting to belabor the point, I came right out and told her that we heard from Council and Cotter was an Eagle Scout. It felt good to say those words and to be able to tell her that Cotter was going to be recognized for all the hard work he put in as a scout. As we talked, I stared out across the valley and appreciated the beautiful scenery that was before me. It was the perfect way to celebrate the news and the beautiful day of hiking I had.

My time in Connecticut allowed me to start to appreciate the beauty of spring and the landscape of New England. Except for the first few miles in Connecticut, I had good weather the entire time I was hiking through it. It only took me 2 1/2 days to get through the state but it was beautiful. Even better, I passed the 1,500-mile mark. For me, that was the psychological three-quarter point. It was Day 99 on the trail and I could feel the time on the trail start to speed up and the miles remaining start to rapidly decrease. When I reached the Massachusetts border, I took a picture at the sign and thought to myself, "only 4 more states to go, 10 states down."

Up to this point on the trail, I was always counting how many miles or other milestones I had accumulated. Now, I was starting to count how many miles and milestones I had left. Like anything else in life, as the end draws near, time seems to speed up and things happen much quicker. The time between resupplies started to pass by quicker and the number of resupplies I had left was dwindling.

When I first set out to hike the AT, I estimated finishing by June 16th. Since I was leaving on January 30th, that gave me 138 days to complete the hike. It was a pretty aggressive time frame, especially considering I was going to turn 50 years old in September. My daily average, including zero-days, was slightly over 15 miles per day. In order to finish by the 16th of June, I was going to have to bring that daily average up. Still ahead of me were the White Mountains in New Hampshire. After hearing all the rumors about how tough the White Mountains were, I knew I needed to make as many miles as I could so I could be ready for a slowdown when I hit the Whites.

Since walking out of Pennsylvania and seeing Laine, the states have been passing by pretty quickly. It had been 11 days since I last saw Laine and I had finished New Jersey, New York, Connecticut, and was hiking in Massachusetts. The weather was fairly decent and everything was greening up. I spent my first night in Sheffield at a hostel and hiking in Massachusetts was not too bad as there were not too many really big climbs. Many of the summits, however, were wooded summits and it was hard to get many views. I covered over 39 miles in my first two full days and had good weather. While stopped talking to a section hiker one morning, two hikers approached from the rear. When they got closer, I saw that it was Bolt and Big Tuna. They had caught up to me. The last time I saw them was two months earlier in Damascus, when I took a zero-day for the snow.

We hiked together for an hour and a half before they stopped to take a break and I continued on. Later in the afternoon, I came across some more subscriber trail magic as a six-pack of Mountain Dew was sitting in a creek on the side of the trail. It was just what I needed as it was mid-afternoon and it was a good time to take a short break before making the final push towards the shelter for the night. I drank one immediately and took one to have later. I made sure to leave the other four for Bolt and Big Tuna as I knew they couldn't be far behind. I had one more climb for the day and then pulled into the shelter just after 5 pm. While I was making dinner, Bolt and Big Tuna joined me and a section hiker at the shelter and we all went to bed pretty early.

Dalton, MA was on the agenda for the next day and I had nearly 12 miles to go to get there. With rain in the forecast and some cool temperatures, I tried to hike as fast as I could not only to beat most of the rain but to keep warm. My body was able to keep warm but when my gloves got wet, my fingers started to freeze. I would take turns pulling my fingers from one hand out of the glove fingers and make a fist while my other gloved hand would hold both of my hiking poles. After a few minutes, my one hand would stop hurting and then I would switch hands. I was able to keep my mind focused on getting to town knowing that I could get a hot shower and a warm dry place to sleep for the night. Add to that some good town food and that was all the motivation I needed to get through the cold rain I was hiking through.

The trail goes through the town of Dalton and I made my way to the Shamrock Village Inn. After getting checked in, I walked to Angelina's which was an Italian place a block or so away. There, I met Roger, a YouTube subscriber of mine who was going to share some information with me on the White Mountains. Roger had hiked a lot in the Whites and he was able to share some information with me on camping and stealth spots. After lunch, I went back to my room and started some laundry and relaxed. For dinner, I went back to Angelina's and also did a small resupply at a gas station.

Leaving Dalton, I started my last full day in Massachusetts. I really had nice weather and put in 20.5 miles, leaving me 600.6 miles away from Katahdin. I passed near a gas station that had a full-service Dunkin Donuts and I made sure to stop and get some food and a Coolatta from the store. Further up the trail, I came across some trail magic by Roger and I took a soda to have with my dinner. After climbing Mt. Greylock, the highest point in the state, I made my way to the next shelter and got the best sleep of my trip thus far.

Waking up under cloudy skies, I hit the trail by 7 am, and before lunch, I crossed into Vermont. When I came across the sign welcoming me to Vermont, it was an emotional moment. I only had three more states to hike through. While Connecticut and Massachusetts were considered the beginning of the New England section of the AT, Vermont would begin to re-introduce me to 4,000-foot summits and some rougher terrain than the last several states. In short, the trail was going to start getting hard again.

The afternoon brought sunshine and also some of the famous mud that Vermont is known for from hikers. Affectionately referred to as "Vermud", there are a lot of areas where boards are placed on the trail in an effort to give hikers somewhere to step without sinking several inches in mud on the trail. The snowmelt from the winter seems to collect on the trail due to the indention the trail causes and that makes it wet with snow or wet with mud. Roots on the trail were also plentiful and as a result, I was only able to average a little over 2 miles per hour hiking. I pushed on as I was scheduled to meet a trail angel named Mike (apparently Mike is a common name for trail angels) who was a Scoutmaster in Bennington. He was going to meet me at the trailhead and take me into town for resupply and a stay at the

Catamount Inn.

I pushed the 21.4 miles to meet him by 6 pm and he took me into town. As he dropped me off at the hotel, he provided me with a bag full of food and scheduled a time to come and get me in the morning to take me back to the trail. Before leaving, he gave me a council shoulder patch from the local Boy Scout Council his troop was a member of and I promised to carry it with me to Katahdin. It was nice to see the Scouting community supporting my hike and it helped to motivate me even more to get to the end.

There was some pretty bad weather coming in the next day and Mike dropped me back off at the trailhead and I started hiking. I was able to hike almost 4 hours before the rain came and it lasted 45 minutes. By the time the rain subsided, I reached a shelter and stopped there to eat some lunch. There were a few section hikers there and we talked as I ate my lunch. They were calling for possible thunderstorms and maybe even tornados but it looked like it would hit where I was later in the afternoon. I decided to push on and try to make it to the next shelter. I ran into some snow on the trail at the higher elevations but since my feet were already wet, I really didn't care too much. The only problem was that the ice-cold water and snow made my feet and toes cold but as long as I kept on hiking, my feet did not hurt too bad.

As the rain slowly started to return, I was getting close to the Story Spring Shelter and the end of my 19-mile day. I pushed hard to avoid getting any wetter than I already was and pulled into the shelter as the rain picked up. I quickly stripped myself of the wet clothes I was wearing and was able to get into some dry clothes and socks that I had in my bag. There is no feeling in the world like hiking 19 miles wet and cold and then being able to put on dry clothes and make a hot meal. The trail teaches you to manage comfort. You really start to appreciate the simple things in life. Things such as dry clothes and a hot meal, even if that meal is Ramen noodles and some tuna, seem like wonderful luxuries when you have been wet and cold all day long.

Stratton Mountain was the big destination on my agenda for Day 107 and after a good night's sleep, I began my trek. Within minutes of getting on the trail, I slipped and took a pretty hard tumble. I picked myself up off the ground, brushed off the dirt that was sticking to my body and continued on. All throughout the hike, I suffered many falls. I was not the most graceful hiker and based on the number of times I fell on the trail, it was obvious I was not becoming any more graceful. Every time I took a spill, the first thought that came to mind was, "is anything hurt?" I had already convinced myself that I was not coming off the trail without touching that sign. The only possible things that could keep me from getting to Katahdin were death, a major illness, a tragedy involving my wife or son, or an injury that I could not hike through or could not recover from in time. Every step I took on the trail could result in disaster. I was learning that a thru-hike required a certain amount of luck.

I reached the summit of Stratton Mountain just in time for lunch. It was sunny and in the 60s, so I had a great place to eat and rest. After catching the view on the top of the fire tower, I sat down at the base of the tower and ate some lunch. I was then able to get a call out to Laine and we talked for a few minutes. When break time was over, I continued on through the mud and occasional snowpack at some of the higher elevations. Later in the afternoon, I was able to call Laine again and talk for 40 minutes while I hiked. All in all, it was turning out to be a good day and after logging 18.3 miles, I pulled into Spruce Peak Shelter which was a fully enclosed cabin. I would end up having the cabin all to myself for the night and I sat eating my dinner thinking about how I was in a cabin in the middle of the Vermont wilderness. I was one lucky guy.

The next day had a couple of big climbs, including Bromley Mountain. While trying to get some water in the morning, I dropped my water filter and it landed on a rock and cracked. I wasn't sure if it would be able to filter after that, so I sent a message to Laine to see what she could do for me. I was not planning on going into town until Rutland and I would not be there until tomorrow afternoon. In the meantime, I would just have to be careful on what streams I drank out of and just pray that I did not get any bad water. Being one of the early hikers of the season, the trails were not very crowded so that meant less chance of contaminated water with fewer hikers on the trail.

By the time I reached the shelter that afternoon, Laine had communicated with a subscriber named Chuck who was willing to bring a filter to me. We tried to coordinate him meeting me at the shelter but it was going to be late that evening, so we opted to meet the next morning at a road crossing. A little after 8 am the next morning, I met up with Chuck who brought me a filter and also some coffee and donuts. I stayed and talked with Chuck for a bit while drinking my coffee and eating some donuts. He lived in the area but had lived in Aiken, SC at one time. Having spent some time in Aiken myself, we talked about how it was funny that the trail brought us together.

Continuing on my hike, I managed several big ups but they were not too bad as I could feel the difference in my stamina and strength. The trail had transformed me into a lean, mean, hiking machine and the nice weather was really keeping my spirits up. I made it to the trailhead leading into the town of Rutland and Laine had coordinated a pick-up for me. Maple, who was about half a day ahead of me, was from Vermont. His Aunt Mary was a subscriber of mine and she volunteered to come and get me from the trailhead, take me to Walmart to resupply, and then drop me off at my hotel. When I reached the trailhead, she was waiting and immediately gave me a Gatorade to drink.

After hitting Walmart for resupply, she dropped me off at the Relax Inn and I thanked her for her help. I did laundry and enjoyed some pizza for dinner. Day 109 was complete and I was sitting at mile marker 1,684.2. There was a Dunkin Donuts right near the hotel, so I picked up myself a donut and coffee after dinner to take back to my room. I already had plans on paying it a visit in the morning to get some breakfast. The weather forecast for the next day was not looking good but since I was trying to make as many miles as I could to hit the June 16th summit date, I was just going to have to get back on the trail and deal with the weather.

The weather held off until 12:30 pm but I was climbing Mt. Killington and had to deal with cold rain and a lot of blow-downs. Being one of the earliest hikers to hit this part of the trail, most trail maintenance crews were not even on the trails cleaning things up from the previous winter yet. That made the climb up Killington cold, wet, and slow. When I reached the top, I came across Cooper Lodge, a stone four-walled shelter that was in pretty bad shape. There was trash all over the floor and even though it had four walls, there were cutouts in the one wall that had plastic covering it. It was 4 pm and I was tired, wet, and freezing. The next shelter was a good 2.5 hours away and was a three-walled shelter. I had cell service here and was unsure if the next shelter would have service. I decided to stay put and get some dry clothes on.

After getting into dry clothes and eating, I pulled out my guide book and tried to plan out the next week or so. Speaking with Laine, we discussed when we were going to be able to get Joe up to hike with me and where I needed to meet him. It started to become clear that I was probably not going to be able to make my June 16th summit goal. At this point in the hike, I was looking forward to getting the trail done and I missed my wife and kid. I did not want to extend my hike any longer than I had to and was feeling pressure to get done by June 16th. Laine kept reassuring me that if it took me longer that was ok but I could not accept that. At the same time, I knew I made the right decision to stop at the shelter as the threat of hypothermia was real. The first thing to be affected by hypothermia is your reasoning and since I was all alone and there were not many other hikers on the trail, staying put was the right thing to do.

As I did four days earlier, getting out of wet clothes and eating some food proved to be exactly what I needed to do. I spent the night alone but was warm, dry, and safe and that was all that mattered. When I woke up and started hiking the next day, it rained for most of the day but eventually stopped later in the afternoon. When I reached the next shelter, I had the company of a section hiker and her dog, Thrilla. I decided to sleep in my damp clothes as my other clothes were still wet from the previous day and the temperatures were not going to get too cold that night. The heat from my body was able to dry out my clothes as I slept.

The sun came out for me the next day and the temperatures warmed up. Spring was here for sure but the trail would bring the occasional rain and cool temperatures just to let me know that while it may be spring, it was definitely not summer yet. There were a good number of ups, some of them pretty steep, but I was able to take advantage of the good weather and I hiked 21.9 miles. That set me up for a short 13.6-mile day the next day and a stay at the Norwich Inn in Norwich. They were calling for intermediate showers and I was able to hike dry until the last 4 miles when a light rain began to fall. At that point, I really did not care too much as a town stop awaited me.

Norwich, VT is right on the Vermont/New Hampshire border and when I left the Inn the next morning, I walked down the sidewalks of Norwich and headed towards the bridge that would carry me over the Connecticut River and into New Hampshire, my 13th state. I called Laine as I hiked along the sidewalk and hung up with her right before the state line so I could video me crossing into New Hampshire. After crossing, I called Laine again to let her know I was another state closer. The trail traveled through Hanover and past Dartmouth College. After a several-mile road hike, the trail took a left into the woods and back up into the mountains.

The weather was nice and I was able to cover 18 miles before stopping at Trapper John Shelter for the night. I was joined by a section hiker named Duck and also ran into two other NOBOs, Peanut Butter and Jelly. PB & J left in early January and had been on and off the trail due to family commitments. I ran into them around lunchtime but they were ahead of me and I could only assume they pushed on to the next shelter. Looking at my guide book, I planned on doing 19 miles the next day to a campsite and actually tent for the first time since I was sick. That would set me up nicely for entering the Whites on the following day.

The closer I got to the Whites, the more anxious I became. For hundreds of miles, all I heard about were the White Mountains. People talk about how tough they are but they also talk about their beauty. When trying to estimate when I could finish my hike, the White Mountains were always the wildcard. Some people say that a 10-mile day in the Whites is a good day. After being used to covering 18-22 miles a day up to this point, it was difficult to imagine the trail being so tough that I would be pulling 10-mile days. I covered the 19 miles to Ore Hill campsite and after tenting that evening, I woke up anxious but ready to attack the Whites.

CHAPTER 15

The Whites

I t was Friday, May 25th and Day 116 on the trail. My plan was to hike 15.5 miles today but they were not just any 15.5 miles. Today would be the day I climbed Mt. Moosilauke and officially entered the Whites. The White Mountains in New Hampshire are, by most accounts, the most beautiful mountains along the Appalachian Trail. They are also some of the most difficult. Granite mountaintops and steep treacherous climbs and descents fill the area. Camping is heavily regulated and more visitors come to the Whites each year than Yellowstone and Yosemite combined. It is also home to Mt. Washington, a place that claims to have some of the worst weather in the world.

The day started out normal as I made my way northbound. I logged about 10 miles and stopped at Jeffers Brook Shelter to eat some lunch. I was only a short distance from the base of Moosilauke so I tried to eat a good lunch and camel up on water. After eating, I started to make my way to the base of the mountain. It is a 5-mile climb covering approximately 3,500 feet. It was sunny and warm when I began my ascent and I would stop every so often to catch my breath and drink some water. I wanted to make sure I was well hydrated so that I would not run low on energy.

As I climbed, the sweat soaked my shirt and shorts but I kept on climbing. Every so often, I would check my Guthooks app to see how far I had climbed. The elevation profile on the app showed a climb that seemed like it just went on forever. The higher I climbed, the more I perspired. Eventually, my shirt and shorts were soaked with sweat and drops of sweat were dripping from the edge of my shorts.

As I got closer to the top, clouds started to roll in and the sun went away. By the time I reached the tree line, the sun was gone and clouds filled the sky. The wind was picking up and with the sweat-soaked clothes I was wearing, I started to get cold. While I was excited to be on the summit of the mountain, the wind and cold combined with the wet clothing I was wearing made the hike very uncomfortable. I pushed on and made it to the summit sign. There were several day hikers at the summit, sitting and taking pictures. When I got there, I took off my pack and retrieved my puffy jacket and put it on to warm up. I had climbed my first mountain in the Whites and I was feeling pretty good.

As I made my way down the mountain, I encountered a pretty rocky descent. I only needed to go a little over 2 miles to get to the Beaver Brook Shelter where I was planning to stay for the night. I reached the shelter and made some dinner. I had cell service so I was able to call Laine and not only tell her I was in the Whites and just climbed Moosilauke, but that I was sitting at mile 1,800. Eventually, I was joined by a section hiker and, after that, PB & J showed up. There was a beautiful view looking out of the front of the shelter but the clouds were rolling in as it was supposed to rain overnight.

Waking up, I packed up and got on the trail by 8 am. I had to hike 1.5 miles down the north side of Moosilauke and it was very slow going. The trail was steep and loaded with rocks and roots. The rain the night before made everything wet and slick. On top of that, there were sections where the trail was essentially a stream. It took me 1 1/2 hours to climb the 1.5 miles down. Fortunately, there was a cooler of trail magic at the base of the mountain and I was able to get a Gatorade. The weather reports were calling for some rain showers in the afternoon and the trail was loaded with roots, rocks, and blowdowns. As I climbed over, under, around, and through the blowdowns, the sharp branches would catch onto my pack and cause me to have to try and unhook myself without tearing holes in my pack.

I was initially planning on covering nearly 18 miles but it became clear very quickly that I was going to be slowed down a lot today and was going to have to re-think my plan. I was wanting to go 18 miles because that would get me to a trailhead and I would be able to get into town for a much-needed resupply. I was out of dinners and only had a little bit of food in my pack. As the day wore on, I could feel the lack of energy in my body. I fell four times as I hiked and even bent one of my trekking poles trying to avoid another fall.

Eventually, I reached the Eliza Creek Shelter at 3 pm and stopped there for the night. It was early but I did not think I could make it up and down South and North Kinsman Mountain and then the long descent down to Interstate 93. I assumed the climb and descent would be just as bad as Moosilauke and it would be dark before getting to the interstate. I decided to stay where I was and do the 9 miles tomorrow and then hit town. I rationed out my food and had enough for a light dinner and breakfast but that would be it.

Physically and mentally, it was the hardest day on the trail thus far. Being wet, hungry, and tired really took a toll on me. Fortunately, I was able to talk to Laine and that made me feel better. I was worried that the lack of food would affect my energy levels and that would make the climb the next day very tough. After spending 2-3 hours alone at the shelter, a retired principal named Hickory arrived. Having someone to talk to was a godsend. As we got into conversation, the worries of the trail started to disappear and the thoughts of having little food started to disappear. Eventually, I laid down to sleep and slept pretty well that night.

When I woke in the morning, I ate my small breakfast and packed up to get ready to go. I started the climb up the Kinsman and tried to keep a steady pace so as not to overwork myself. My legs felt better than the day before and I made it up the mountain without getting worn out. There were a lot of rocks, roots, and blowdowns that added to the wet and soggy trail. When I started down, I knew it would be long and slow but, mentally, I knew it was literally all downhill from this point to the interstate. In a little over 5 miles, I would be picked up and taken to a hotel. I kept that thought in my mind and just continued pushing. Eventually, after 7 hours of hiking, I finished the 8.8 miles for the day and met up with the hotel owner who drove me to the hotel. After a shower, resupply, laundry, and two meals, I was all back to normal and ready to get some sleep so I could head back out into the Whites the next day.

Having the time in the hotel that night, I was able to look ahead on the trail and do some planning. The Whites are different than any other section of the trail not only because the terrain is different, but also because the camping is different. There are a lot of sections of the trail in the Whites that run above tree line. In those areas, the terrain consists of granite and sporadic alpine vegetation. This vegetation is very fragile and if trampled on can easily die and it takes decades to grow back. For this reason, camping above tree line is forbidden in the Whites. The Appalachian Mountain Club (AMC), which maintains the trail in the Whites, run a series of huts that are spaced roughly 10 miles apart. Reservations in these huts are not only hard to get and must be made months in advance, but they are very expensive. They do offer some work-for-stay options to thru-hikers but since I was arriving so early in the season, the huts were not opening until the end of the week.

There are some campsites and shelters but they charge $10

to camp. Fortunately, since the huts were not open yet, the shelters did not have caretakers there and they were not charging. I planned to do another lighter day of just over 10 miles, since I had a big climb right out of the gate this morning. After that, I would hike Franconia Ridge and Little Haystack, Mount Lincoln, and Mt. Lafayette. After a cloudy start to the morning and dozens and dozens of blowdowns heading up to Franconia Ridge, the rest of the day was sunny and beautiful. I especially enjoyed eating my lunch on Mt. Lincoln with some day hikers that were there.

I had a pretty long descent before a very steep climb up Mt. Garfield. The climbs up the mountains in the Whites were typically pretty steep climbs. Some were not long climbs but they definitely covered some big elevation gains. It was not unusual to climb 1,000 feet per mile in the Whites and there were no such things as switchbacks in New England. A switchback is where the trail is built in a zigzag so that the grade is more gradual. These are very popular in the South but in New England, and especially in the Whites, the trail goes straight up. I remember hiking down south and as I climbed up a switchback, I could see the top of the mountain and would get frustrated because the switchback made it longer to get to the summit. I would say to myself, "I can see the top, why can't I just go straight up?" Now that I was in the Whites and the trail did go straight up, I was longing for a switchback.

After summiting Garfield, I started the rocky descent and took the spur trail to the shelter. I got there pretty early but it gave me a chance to relax and rest up. I met a section hiker from Canada and, a little while later, a couple of hikers from Belgium showed up. I thought it was pretty funny that I was the only American at the shelter that night but it just showed how popular the Whites really are to hikers from all over the world.

I planned on putting in a 14.6-mile day the next day and I was able to get on the trail by 7:15 am. Since I was getting further north and the days were getting longer, the sun was rising earlier in the morning and I was getting on the trail earlier. The descent from Garfield was crazy as the trail was essentially a creek covered with wet rocks. I carefully placed each step, making sure I had solid footing before shifting my weight onto that foot. Doing so took time and was mentally exhausting. I spent most of my time throughout the day having to stare at my feet to see where my feet were going.

After a steep, tough climb up South Twin Mountain and soaking my clothes in sweat, the rest of the day was mostly downs and straights which was a nice change of pace from the last several days. I pushed on to Ethan Pond Shelter and arrived there at 4:30 pm. Another early day but I did cover the 14.6 miles I was hoping to do. One of the reasons I was not upset with stopping a little early the last few days was the upcoming weather. I had been watching the weather and trying to coordinate my hiking so that I had a good day to summit Mt. Washington.

Mt. Washington is notorious for bad weather and, in some cases, deadly weather. Just earlier in the year, there was a day in January where the temperature with the wind chill hit -100 degrees Fahrenheit. It was Tuesday and we were expected to have beautiful weather on Wednesday and Thursday. Since I was 14 miles from Lake of the Clouds Hut, my plan was to hike those 14 miles on Wednesday and stay at the hut Wednesday night. There was a room in the bottom of the hut known as the Dungeon and it had 6 bunks and thru-hikers were allowed to stay there for $10. That would put me at the base of Mt. Washington and I could summit first thing Thursday morning and have a beautiful day to hike the Presidential range.

According to the trail guide, the huts were not supposed to open until June 1st, which was Friday. The "cru" which were the workers at the huts, were already at the huts getting them ready to open for the season. I messaged Laine and asked her to call in the morning to see if the Dungeon at Lake of the Clouds was open so that I could stay there. Lake of the Clouds was above tree line so there was no camping allowed. You either had to do work-for-stay or stay in the dungeon. Since the hut was not officially open yet, work-for-stay would not be an option so the Dungeon would be my only shot. If the Dungeon was not open, I would have to stop at Mizpah Hut which was 5 miles before Mt. Washington.

The shelter at Ethan Pond was full as there were six of us there plus several people tenting. Most were section hikers but there was another NOBO named Small Furry Animal. It was the most people I had to share a shelter with on the entire trail but it wasn't too bad. I was on one of the ends and had a section hiker next to me who was an older gentleman near my age. All the rest were hikers in their 20s. Not long after it got dark and we all tried to go to sleep, the guy next to me started snoring really loud. Fortunately, I had some earbuds and I put them in my ears and pulled out my iPod to listen to some music. When I woke up a few hours later and got up to use the bathroom, he had stopped snoring but as soon as I got back under my quilt, he started again and I had to put the earbuds back in.

In the morning, I got on the trail by 7:20 am and hiked for 3 miles before starting the big climb up Mt. Webster. While hiking up the mountain I received a message from Laine that Lake of the Clouds was not open yet and I could not stay at the Dungeon. I really wanted to be able to stay there and it was a beautiful day to hike, so this was disappointing news. When I reached the top of Webster, I stopped and ate some lunch. I tried to call Laine but she was at work and busy. As I sat on the top of Webster, I could see Mizpah Hut and, far in the distance, Mt. Washington. I decided I would hike on to Mitzpah and figure out what to do when I got there. I messaged Laine and told her I would probably have to tent there and just summit Mt. Washington a little later the next day.

After summiting Mt. Jackson, I descended and started climbing Mt. Pierce and arrived at Mizpah Hut. I went into the hut and filled up my water bottles. I approached one of the Cru members and asked about a tenting spot. She explained they were $10 and I told her that I was planning on staying at Lake of the Clouds but my wife was told that the Dungeon was closed. Before I could say anymore, another Cru member came in and the first one explained to the second one what I was trying to do. He tried to send a text to Lake of the Clouds but he could not get it to go through. He told me that it was a beautiful day and it was too nice of a day to stop at 3 pm. I agreed. He told me that he worked at Lake of the Clouds the year before and the Dungeon still might be frozen up from the winter. It was not unusual for the Dungeon to fill with ice over the winter and it took a while to melt. He told me I could try and see if I could stay there and if not, I could see if they would let me sleep on the floor in the hut.

If they said no, I might have to hike back the 5 miles to Mizpah as the trail between here and there is almost all above tree line, so no camping is allowed. I looked at the beautiful weather outside, looked at my watch, and said screw it. I put my pack back on and headed back onto the trail. I wasn't sure this was the right thing to do but I was committed at this point and only time would tell if it was the right decision.

The above tree line hike was beautiful as I made my way to Lake of the Clouds. As I hiked, I could see the mighty Mt. Washington in the distance and, little by little, it got bigger in my view. I kept praying that they would let me stay somewhere in or out of the hut. I also thought about Laine. The last she knew, I was going to tent at Mizpah. If she were to pull up my Garmin track on the computer, she would see that I already passed Mizpah. Sure enough, I received a Garmin text message asking me where I was going. I responded that I was going to chance it.

Eventually, Lake of the Clouds was visible and I pushed

harder to get there as quickly as I could. Finally, at 5:30 pm I arrived at the hut and walked in the front door. Inside there were a group of Cru members setting up tables and trying to get things ready for the opening the following day. I stood there quietly and waited for someone to acknowledge my presence and ask what I wanted. Finally, a young lady asked if she could help me and I asked her if the Dungeon was open. "Yes, it's $10 for the night." Excited to hear this, I immediately asked where I could pay. I reached into my pocket and pulled out a ten-dollar bill and offered it to her. She took the money and told me where to go. She also told me there were already 2 hikers in there.

I walked back outside and around to the side of the hut and ran into Hickory and Small Furry Animal. I greeted both of them and told them I was going to be joining them for the night. I walked into the small concrete room and was careful to watch my step as half of the concrete floor had a one-inch thick covering of ice. There were two wooden bunk beds that were three bunks high with a simple piece of plywood as the mattress. I chose one of the top bunks and set up my stuff. After doing so, I joined the others who were sitting right outside the metal door that secured the Dungeon and began to cook my dinner.

As we all sat and ate, I was able to get a call out to Laine and explained to her what had happened. It was a beautiful evening and the weather was not that cold. As I sat there staring up at Mt. Washington, I felt so grateful that I was able to get to the hut and have a place to stay. I was even more grateful that I would be able to summit Mt. Washington first thing in the morning and the weather was looking great for the hike. As we sat there talking, a Cru member came out to us and asked if we wanted some nachos. They had made some but made more than they could eat. All three of us looked at each other and then responded, "absolutely!" She should have known better than to ask one thru-hiker, let alone three, whether or not they wanted food.

A few minutes later, she brought out a baking tray that was two-foot by two-foot and covered with nachos, corn, ground beef, and cheese. Some of the chips were a little burnt but we didn't care. We sat there together and cleaned up the entire tray. It was a cool evening but not cold. As we sat there, we watched the sun sink into the sky and illuminate into one of the most beautiful sunsets I have ever seen. I thought to myself how lucky I was to be where I was and I was getting excited for the summit of Washington in the morning.

When we all crawled into our bunks that night and closed the large metal door, sealing ourselves in the Dungeon, I laid back and felt grateful for being able to get to where I was at. I was cozy in my quilt and it was nice to see some familiar faces when I arrived at the hut. I dozed off to sleep and slept pretty comfortably that evening.

We all got up the next morning and ate a simple breakfast. We were all ready to get up the mountain before all the tourists started to arrive for the day. By 7:30 am, I was on the trail and making my way up the mountain. It was a rocky climb as I was pretty much stepping on rocks the entire way up. I don't think my feet ever stepped onto actual dirt, it was all rocks. Finally, at 8:30 am, I reached the top. Within just a few minutes, Small Furry Animal and Hickory also made it up and we headed for the summit sign to get our pictures taken. It was a beautiful sunny morning without a cloud in the sky and no wind. The temperature was about 50 degrees. I could not ask for a better day to be on top of Mt. Washington. Especially since tomorrow was calling for thunderstorms. We went into the snack bar on top and got a snack and relaxed for a while.

After an hour or so at the summit, Small Furry Animal and I headed out over the Presidentials. The Presidentials are a series of above tree line summits that are probably the most beautiful views in the Whites. For several miles, we hiked on nothing but granite rocks. For several hours, we hiked, trying to get to the end and get back below tree line so our feet could feel actual ground again. Eventually, we made the long descent into Pinkham Notch and met a shuttle driver at the Visitor's Center. Laine had already arranged for me to stay at the Rattle River Hostel in Gorham, and while we were hiking, I convinced Small Furry Animal to join me. After being picked up, we hit the Walmart for resupply and then were taken to the hostel and checked into our rooms.

The only thing that separated me from finishing the Whites was one more 21-mile section consisting of the Wildcats, Carter, and Mt. Moriah. The weather was not going to be the best the next day but Small Furry Animal

felt just like I did, we wanted to be done with the Whites and we made a plan to do the entire 21 miles in one day. Our plan was to carry our packs but leave most of our food back at the hostel. We would take just enough food to last a day and a half.

If we could not make the 21 miles in one day, we would camp and then finish the mileage on the second day and stay another night at the hostel. If we did cover all 21 miles, then we would spend that night at the hostel.

The hostel owner was skeptical about whether we would make it in one day but we were committed to doing it if at all possible. We were dropped off at 7:30 am and immediately had one of the steepest climbs on the AT. We pushed ourselves and took very few breaks. We would drink as we hiked and hiked in and out of several rain showers. Around lunchtime, we reached Carter Notch Hut and stopped there for a 45-minute lunch break. After lunch, we continued on and pushed ourselves. The terrain was tough but by mid-afternoon, we decided that we were going the entire way. Our goal was to just try and beat nightfall. We pushed and pushed as the hours went by and so did the miles. We were wet, tired, and hungry. Finally, after 13 hours of hiking, we came walking back in the driveway of the Rattle River hostel at 8:30 pm just as the sun was going down.

I was tired and still needed to shower and grab some dinner but the Whites were done and I had survived. Tomorrow, I would hike into the fourteenth and final state, Maine.

CHAPTER 16

Entering Maine

I woke up in New Hampshire for the very last time. If everything went according to plan, I would cross into Maine before the end of the day. Due to the long hiking day yesterday and getting to bed late, I took my time in the morning eating breakfast and getting everything ready to go. I headed out a little after 9 am and made my way towards the Maine border. The terrain wasn't too bad but it did include some big ups and a fair share of blowdowns. I hiked alone all day as Small Furry Animal headed out before me and planned on going further. My plan was to go 17 miles to the first shelter just over the Maine border.

I felt pretty good hiking, considering the long, hard day yesterday, but the terrain was still rough and with the blowdowns. It was tough to keep a good pace going. Late in the afternoon, I summited Mount Success, the last mountain I would summit in New Hampshire. Eventually, around 7 pm, deep in the woods I came across a simple white sign that announced my entry into Maine. For over 1,900 miles, whenever someone would ask me where I was headed, I would respond simply, "Maine". For the first time in four months, I could now say "Katahdin". I stood alone in the woods next to the sign and tried to take my own picture. Just like most of my journey up to this point, I was all alone and there was no fanfare. While I was happy that I had made it this far, I knew there was still more I needed to accomplish on this journey.

After sending a Garmin text to my wife to let her know that I had reached Maine, I pushed forward to get to the shelter before nightfall. Not too much later, I reached the spur trail that would take me to the shelter. The shelter was 0.3 miles off the AT which, on Guthooks, did not strike me as anything unusual. What I found out, however, was most of that was a rock scramble. As I maneuvered up and over the rocks, I thought to myself, what a hell of a way to be welcomed to Maine. I knew right there that even though The Whites were behind me, the trail wasn't going to get any easier. I finally reached the shelter and hurried to filter some water and cook dinner before the sun went down. After cleaning up and securing my food in the bear box, I laid down in the shelter and tried to rest up for the next day.

I was only 5 miles away from Mahoosuc Notch, the toughest mile on the entire Appalachian Trail. It is a series of boulders that create a "boulder jungle gym" that goes on for nearly a mile. Hikers have to squeeze over, around and under boulders and also have to jump from boulder to boulder in order to navigate this section. It is not uncommon for there to be ice and snow even in August. After getting out of the notch, NOBOs are then faced with the Mahoosuc Arm, which is an extremely steep climb out of the notch.

When I woke up the next morning, I could feel the accumulation of the tough miles I hiked in The Whites. From everything I had heard, southern Maine was going to be every bit as tough, if not tougher. I made it to a shelter around lunchtime and stopped there to eat my lunch. Due to all the roots and rocks in the trail, I was only averaging a little over one mile per hour. I remember the shuttle driver that picked us up at Pinkham Notch telling me how bad the roots were in Maine. From what I experienced this morning, he was correct. The best way I could describe the roots in Maine is to imagine a large cargo net. That is what the ground looked like in Maine. It was a huge "cargo net" of roots - small, medium and large ones.

After eating lunch, I headed down the trail and into the Notch. As I stared ahead in the trail, it looked like someone had just dumped boulders the size of cars in a big pile right in front of me. There was no way to go around this boulder field. You just had to navigate through it. In the beginning, as I started maneuvering through the Notch, it wasn't too bad. I was the only person around so I had to evaluate where I would step and how I would make my way to the next blaze. On some of the rocks, there would be blazes, and on others, there would be arrows to show you the way to go. There was still some snow and ice on some of the rocks and down in the crevices between the rocks. At times, you had to jump from one rock to the other, being careful not to fall down into the crevice where other rocks, snow and ice existed.

It was more mentally challenging than physically challenging for me, as all I kept thinking about was not falling or doing anything to get hurt. One wrong move and you could fall several feet down into a crevice and onto rocks. My trip and possibly more than that could end at any moment. At one point, while trying to creep along one side of a boulder, I lost my balance and started to fall backwards. I reached my arm back and was able to grab hold of another boulder and stop myself from tumbling head first, backwards. I stood there suspended for a few moments while I composed my thoughts and slowly continued on.

When I got about 3/4 of the way through the Notch, I started to second guess myself and tried to remember the last time I saw a white blaze. I tried to check my positioning on Guthooks but I was getting crazy readings, most likely because I was hidden in all of these boulders. I decided to backtrack to the last white blaze I could find to make sure I was still on the trail. After backtracking for 15 minutes, I found a white blaze and then turned around and started north again through the Notch.

As I was headed back North, I came to a spot where I had to jump off of one boulder down to the ground three feet below. When I jumped, my left foot hit the ground first and my ankle rolled. When the ankle rolled, all of my body weight came down on it and I heard a snap. I caught myself with my trekking pole and stopped myself from falling by leaning on a rock. I lifted my left foot off the ground and stood on my right foot as pain shot through my left ankle. My first thought was that I had broken my ankle and my hike was done. I took several deep breaths, waiting for some of the pain to subside. After about a minute, most of the pain was gone and I slowly put my left foot back on the ground to see if I could put any weight back on the ankle. It was sore but I could put weight on it. A feeling of relief came over me knowing that I would be able to continue on but I did worry that it might swell over time. For the time being, I couldn't worry about that. Eventually, I ended up at the same place I turned around and I just assumed that I still must be on the trail but just hadn't seen a blaze in a while. I continued forward and, eventually, the boulders started to disappear and I was back out on the trail.

When I looked down at my watch, it had taken me nearly 3 hours to go 0.8 miles through the Notch. Having to backtrack cost me at least 30 minutes. It wasn't long before I hit the bottom of the Mahoosuc Arm and started to climb. It was a short 1700-foot climb and it was steep. I would push myself for a minute or two and then stop for 30 seconds to catch my breath. I kept repeating this until, finally, I reached the top. Speck Pond Shelter was a mile from the top of the Arm and that is where I decided to stay for the night. Even though it would give me only a 9-mile day, Mahoosuc Notch and Arm would be behind me.

When I arrived, there were about 15-20 Canadian college students with their professor and his wife at the shelter. All of the students were staying in tents and only the professor and his wife were in the shelter. When I arrived, the professor made the students clear some space for me and they even offered me food and water. As I ate, I chatted with them some and since it was getting close to dark, we all started to get ready to go to bed. The weather forecast for the next day was not looking good. It was supposed to rain all day and the temperatures were not supposed to get above 38 degrees. In addition to that, they were calling for 40mph winds and I would have to spend at least half of my day above the tree line. I really was not looking forward to the next day. I decided that I had had a long, tough day today and that I would just get some sleep and worry about tomorrow, when I woke up.

When I woke up in the morning, I was treated to a Mountain House breakfast meal by one of the students and they even filtered water for me. The professor had actually hiked most of the AT in Maine and was familiar with the section I was about to hike. After speaking with him and talking to Laine, I decided to take a zero-day at the shelter. The weather was going to be much better the following day and I was worried that while I might be able to stay warm while I was hiking, I would not have dry clothes to put on after hiking all day and with the cold temperatures, I could risk hypothermia. On top of that, I had not had a day off in 600 miles and I had earned it.

My son, Joe, was planning to come and hike with me here in Maine. The plan was for him to fly to Portland, ME where he would be picked up by some friends of ours that live nearby. They would then bring him to meet with me on Saturday wherever I was going to be. After looking at the guidebook and talking to Laine, it was decided that the best place to meet would be in Rangeley, ME. It was only 52 miles away and if I took today off, that would give me 5 days to get there. We decided that I could stay at Pine Ellis Hostel in Andover, ME and slack-pack for several days which would allow me to meet Joe on Saturday afternoon. Since I only had about 270 miles left on the trail, it was time for me to slow down and savor the last few weeks. By staying in Andover for a few nights, I would be able to hike 10-13 miles each day and eat a lot of food. Since I had lost about 50 pounds so far on the trail and was low on energy, this seemed like a good plan.

While Laine spent the morning making reservations with the hostel and coordinating Joe's trip with our friends in Maine, I laid back down and took a four-hour nap while the wind and rain beat down on the shelter. When I woke up around lunchtime, I ate some food and talked to Laine on the phone. It was nice to get some extra sleep but it was also a little boring being all alone in a shelter, all day long. Later in the afternoon, the rain stopped and I went and filtered water. By dinner, the wind had died down and the weather was starting to clear.

The next morning, I got up and headed up and over Speck Mountain and headed down to Grafton Notch. I only had to hike 4.6 miles before meeting David from Pine Ellis Hostel at the parking lot. He took me back to Andover where I was able to get settled in the hostel and eat lunch in town. It was Tuesday afternoon and my plan was to stay at the hostel for four nights until Saturday morning. David was going to slack-pack me on Wednesday, Thursday and Friday, allowing me to cover 10-13 miles each day. I would then be able to eat some good town food every day and sleep in a nice bed every night. On Saturday morning, he would drop me off for the last time and I would hike the final 13 miles to meet Joe.

During my week at Pine Ellis, I was able to meet several other NOBOs as they arrived at the hostel. Among some of them were PB & J, who I had last seen at the beginning of the Whites. Slowing down and taking it easy this week was exactly what my body and mind needed. I was able to rest, recover and eat a lot of food, helping to increase my energy levels. On top of all that, each and every day that went by brought me that much closer to being reunited with Joe. For weeks, I had counted down to the day when he would be with me and I would have a buddy to hike with. He was planning on hiking for 9 days with me, all the way to Monson, ME and the beginning of the 100 Mile wilderness.

On Friday, after finishing my last slack-pack session, I washed all of my clothes and packed all of my stuff in my backpack. I would spend one more night at the hostel and then head out at 7 am with David for the last time. That evening, I walked over to The Big Red Hen and had Prime Rib for dinner. It was delicious and was the perfect last supper before seeing Joe. I was the only hiker staying at the hostel that night so I had the room all to myself and I fell asleep watching TV and dreaming about what it would feel like to see Joe the next day.

I got up early the next morning and got dressed. I made sure my pack was all ready to go and then I walked downstairs into the kitchen and poured myself a cup of coffee. I sat down at the table to drink my coffee and eat my muffin. After breakfast, I got my pack and headed out the front door to retrieve my poles and shoes from the porch. David came out and we got in the car and headed towards the trail. It was a 45-minute drive to get to the trailhead and David and I talked the entire way. When we finally pulled up to the trailhead, I retrieved my pack and poles and thanked David for all the help over the past week.

I stepped back onto the trail with a renewed purpose. I felt refreshed and rejuvenated and I wanted to hike the next 13 miles as quickly as possible. I put in my earbuds and pulled out my iPod and listened to music as I hiked. The trail to Rangeley was fairly flat with just minor ups and downs. According to David, it was a fairly easy section and I should be able to make good time. It was a beautiful day to hike and everything was going well. Each hour, I would check my position and I was hiking at a good 2.5-3.0 mph pace.

Before I knew it, I arrived at the parking lot at Route 4 and announced my arrival. Off to the left, I saw my son walking across the parking lot to greet me. We hugged each other and then I greeted my friend, Mike, and his son, Christopher, who brought Joe to me. We hung out in the parking lot for a while and ate some lunch that Mike had packed in for us. We ate lobster rolls and had a beer. After eating and hanging out for a while, we got Joe's pack out of the car and got ready to leave our friends and hike on to the next shelter.

Joe and I headed off into the woods and hiked 1.5 miles to the Piazza Rock Shelter and set up camp. It was really nice to have him with me and I was excited and looking forward to the next nine days. We were the only ones at the shelter and made ourselves at home. After setting up, we relaxed and talked for a while before making some dinner. Fortunately, Joe had experience backpacking and I was excited to introduce him to the AT and, in particular, Maine. As we lay down to sleep, we were just about to doze off when two hikers arrived at the shelter. As they settled in for the night, I rolled over and attempted to sleep. Eventually, within 30 minutes of their arrival, they were bedding down and going to sleep.

Even though it was June, the evening and morning temperatures were still cool. Our fellow hikers got up before we did and headed out. Joe and I took our time getting ready. I had planned for us to cover around 17 miles today. In the morning, we climbed up Saddleback, The Horn, and Saddleback Jr. Joe got to experience what it was like to hike up and out of the woods and get above the tree line. As soon as we emerged from the trees, we could feel the cold wind as it hit our sweat-soaked shirts. The view was spectacular and was worth the climb. We were able to eat our lunch on top of Saddleback Jr. before attacking a bunch of rocky downs in the afternoon.

As we neared the end of the day and got within a mile of the shelter, we started to hit blowdown after blowdown. We passed a section hiker a couple of hours before that who warned us that there were a lot of blowdowns up ahead. Apparently, he was correct. After hiking 16 pretty tough miles, the AT threw us the blowdowns. Joe got a good taste of what I had encountered up to this point. Finally, we made it to the shelter and looked forward to a hot meal and a good night's sleep. We were sitting at mile 1989.2, which meant I was only 200.7 miles from the top of Katahdin.

Day 133 greeted us with some beautiful weather and some big milestones. The plan was to hike 13.5 miles into Stratton and stay at the Stratton Inn and resupply. It would be Joe's first town stop and I was looking forward to hanging out in town with him. We had to hike North and South Crocker Mountains but, more importantly, I was going to cross over the 2,000-mile mark. Before I could get close to it, I rolled the same ankle that I injured at Mahoosuc Notch but, fortunately, I was able to walk on it without too much pain. As we were making our descent down into Stratton, I kept my eye on Guthooks as I drew closer and closer to the 2,000-mile mark. I was in the lead and Joe was right on my tail as we navigated the rocks and roots on our way down. I was so focused on getting to that milestone that I failed to lift my foot far enough off the ground and my toe hooked under a root that was protruding from the trail and sent me face first onto the ground. As I was landing on the ground, my left knee slammed hard onto another root that was traversing the trail. I let out a yell and rolled onto my side.

I grabbed my knee and tried to hold my breath, hoping the pain would subside. Joe asked if I was ok and I told him I thought so. After giving my leg a chance to stop hurting, Joe helped me to my feet and I brushed myself off. After 2,000 miles, I was frustrated and getting tired of falling on my face. Since entering Maine, I had some pretty hard falls and ankle rolls, and with each one, I worried I would injure myself badly enough to end my hike. Fortunately, someone was looking out for me and protecting me from getting injured.

Finally, I looked over to my left and I saw it. On the side of the trail, spelled out in sticks, was the number 2,000. "There it is!" I exclaimed to Joe and I walked over and stared at the ground. As I stared at the homemade trail marker on the ground, I couldn't help but think of the 2,000-mile marker I saw back in the Smokies. Back then, I remember wondering what SOBOs thought when they came across that sign. Now I knew. I thought about the sheer vastness of the number. I thought about how in the beginning it was hard to comprehend a number that large. Now, standing and staring at those sticks, I realized that I had reached that number by just following a simple rule… keep pushing north. Every step I took brought me closer to that number.

There were no tears, there were no exclamations of joy. I handed my phone to Joe and told him to get a picture of me standing by the sign. He took the picture and congratulated me as he handed me back my phone. I put the phone back in my pocket and resumed heading north. That was it. Much like the sign at the Maine border, there was no fanfare and just a brief photo opportunity. I was happy, I was proud, but I was not done. The only sign that meant anything was the one standing atop of Baxter Peak on Katahdin.

We pushed forward the next couple of miles and reached the road crossing where we would meet the shuttle driver to take us into Stratton. We checked into the Inn and took showers before grabbing a Wolf Burger at the White Wolf Inn and then resupplying. We had the Bigelows awaiting us after our town stay so we tried to eat some good food and get some rest.

A 15-mile day and the Bigelows awaited us when we left Stratton and the views did not disappoint. All of the summits were above the tree line and with the clear skies and beautiful weather I could see for what seemed like forever. We climbed up and down over a series of peaks before lunch and stopped at a campsite to eat some lunch and take a nice break. After lunch, we climbed Avery Peak before a long rocky descent took us to the base of Little Bigelow Mountain and our last climb of the day. After summiting, we descended a good portion to Little Bigelow Lean-To and stopped there for the night.

I really enjoyed hiking with Joe as I had someone to talk to on occasion and someone to eat lunch and dinner with during the day. Typically, we would both have our earbuds in listening to music but would take them out and talk whenever one of us had something to say. We kept a good pace hiking and although Joe did not have 2,000 miles under his belt, he was only 17 years old and had no problem keeping up with me. Being able to spend 24 hours a day together without interruptions from anyone else was nice. I was hiking through some of the most beautiful parts of the trail, with beautiful weather, and I had my son there with me. I could not think of a better time. This time with Joe made the entire trip worth it.

We were planning a 17.7-mile day on Wednesday and it would be the longest mileage day for Joe and I. Even though it was the longest as far as mileage was concerned, it looked to have some pretty decent terrain. There were only two ups and a lot of fairly level terrain. We wanted to make it to Pierce Pond Lean-To and stay there for the night because that would leave us with just 4 miles to do the next morning to catch the ride across the Kennebec River. As we hiked, we ran into a guy who was speaking to some SOBOs. We would later learn that he was a NOBO named Dragon. As the afternoon went on, we wound up passing each other several times until we all ended the day at the shelter by 3:30 pm.

The shelter is located right on the shores of Pierce Pond. In Maine, they have dozens of "ponds" along the AT. These ponds, although they sound small and quaint, are actually large bodies of water. Pierce Pond serves as the water source for hikers staying at the shelter and in the evening as the sun is setting over the horizon of the pond, you can hear the loons start to call. It was with this backdrop that Joe and I relaxed at the shelter talking with Dragon and a section hiker. Dragon had recently retired from a long career in the Air Force and when asked about his trail name, he would say, "I'm dragging in the morning and I'm dragging in the evening."

In the morning, we had a short 4 miles to get to the Kennebec River and meet the canoe ferry that shuttles hikers across. The river is too deep and dangerous to try to ford, so hikers are supposed to use the ferry. We then had plans to stay in Caratunk which was on the other side of the river. Joe and I were on the trail by 7 am and headed towards the Kennebec hoping to get there around 9 am to catch the canoe shuttle early. It was not a bad stretch of trail and we arrived shortly after 9 and waited on the shoreline as the canoe was on the other side picking up some SOBOs. When he returned, we put on lifejackets and got into the canoe, placing our packs in the center. Joe took the bow and grabbed a paddle as I sat in the middle and the ferry operator manned the stern and steered. Within just a few minutes, we were safely on the other side and got out of the canoe.

It was a short half-mile hike to the Caratunk Bed and Breakfast and we arrived and made contact with the owner, Paul. He was a former thru-hiker of not only the AT but also the Pacific Crest Trail. According to the guidebook, the place was known for old-fashioned milkshakes and Joe and I made sure we got one within minutes of arriving. In addition, he also made us each a pulled pork sandwich and we ate it as our laundry was being done. Dragon had stopped in for a snack and some resupply but then hiked on. After taking showers, Joe and I relaxed for the rest of the day before hitting town for dinner that evening. In the afternoon, the rain came and we were both happy that we were taking the rest of the day off and did not have to hike in it.

It was nice to be able to relax and hang out with Joe but it would be the last town stay for the two of us together. We had just under 37 miles to go before we got to Monson where Joe would be picked up to return home. The plan was to hike almost 15 miles, leaving Caratunk the next day and then do 13 miles the following day. Our final day together would be 9 miles, putting us in Monson by lunch on the third day. Weather was supposed to be beautiful all three days and I was looking forward to it.

Breakfast was cooked by Paul and it included eggs, bacon, home fries, and blueberry muffins. In addition, fresh ground coffee made it a great breakfast. We were able to get back on the trail around 9 am and hiked for a couple of hours before we saw someone ahead in the trail. As we got closer, I could see a guy that was sitting in a chair next to his truck that was located on a roadbed. As he saw us approach, he got up from his chair and called out my name. His name was Jim and he had slept in the chair all night long hoping to run into us. We stopped and chatted with him and he shared some Ginger Ale and snacks with us. It was a nice surprise to run into some trail magic and it was Joe's first experience of trail magic.

After taking a break with Jim, we continued on, climbing our one peak of the day and eating our lunch on top. We then ran into a hiker named One Way who was hiking in honor of Veteran Suicide Awareness and he gave Joe and I a bracelet and dog tags for awareness. It was really cool to run into others on the trail and spend some time speaking with them, however, I was definitely starting to get the feeling that the trip was coming to an end. Fortunately, the trail was giving me great weather and beautiful views to share with Joe. Even though the trail was full of rocks and roots, the sights, sounds, and smells were amazing. At the shelter that night, we met a SOBO hiker and also another NOBO hiker named Pizza Hut. He was actually doing a flip flop, starting in Virginia near where he lived and hiking north to Katahdin and then going back to where he started in Virginia and hiking south all the way to Springer.

On Saturday, we got on the trail by 8 am and started our last full day of hiking together. We only had 13 miles to cover and we took our time. We had one good climb in the morning and the rest of the day was either fairly flat or downhill. We stopped at the summit of Moxie Bald and enjoyed a nice break. There were several SOBOs doing the same and we talked with them for a while. Over the last several days, we were constantly running into SOBOs as the initial bubble of them were making their way from Katahdin and through the 100-mile wilderness. While it was nice to see other people, all I could think about was getting to Katahdin and getting home to see Laine.

We saw Pizza Hut a few times during the day but when we reached the shelter, it was still early, around 3:30 pm. We only had 9 more miles to get to Monson but our plan was to relax and enjoy arriving early at the shelter. We thought that we might see Pizza Hut but as it got later in the afternoon, we assumed he kept hiking to Monson. It was our last night on the trail together and Joe and I had the shelter all to ourselves. Since I would be able to resupply the next day and Joe was going home, we sat and ate whatever we had in our food bag, saving just enough food for breakfast and a few snacks. It was Saturday night and we had our own private shelter in the Maine wilderness.

Being so far north meant that the sun rises early in the morning. We both got up from our sleeping bags and started our morning routine. It was Father's Day and getting to spend most of the day with Joe was the best way to celebrate it. We packed up and got on the trail by 7 am. We began the 9-mile hike to Monson and enjoyed another great weather day. Over the past 9 days with Joe, we could not have had better weather. The only time we had rain was either overnight when we were asleep, or the one day when we beat the rain to Caratunk. The trail was rewarding me for sticking out all the tough times and was now allowing me to enjoy and share the trail with Joe.

We covered the 9 miles in less than four hours and arrived at the trailhead at Route 15. I messaged Laine and she contacted Shaw's Hiker Hostel and they sent a shuttle to come and get us. Within a few minutes, we were picked up and taken to the hostel. The plan was for our friends to meet us at the hostel and then take Joe back with them to their home near Portland. He was scheduled to fly home the next day so he could get ready to start his summer job in New Jersey. Laine had booked me a private room and I put my pack in the room and Joe and I went outside to the backyard to relax.

There were several SOBOs who had just gotten out of the 100-mile wilderness and they would be spending the night. In addition to some SOBOs, Pizza Hut and Dragon were also at the hostel. An hour or so after arriving, Mike and his wife, Ann Marie, pulled into the driveway. They brought some sandwiches for lunch and we sat around and ate while we filled them in on the adventures of the past 9 days. It was a beautiful sunny day and a perfect day to sit outside and enjoy a lazy Sunday afternoon with great friends.

After lunch, we walked a few blocks over to the Visitor's Center where we were able to talk to them about the 100 Mile Wilderness and Baxter State Park. The employees there were able to answer questions about how to navigate through Baxter State Park and helped me plan how to get picked up after summiting Katahdin. I was only 114.5 miles from the top of Katahdin and I would be entering the 100 Mile Wilderness first thing tomorrow morning. According to my plan, I would finish the Wilderness on Friday, stay at Abol Campground, then hike 10 miles on Saturday into Baxter and camp at Katahdin Stream Campground that night. On Sunday, I would do my summit of Katahdin and Mike and Ann Marie would meet me back at the bottom to take me home with them on Sunday afternoon. Laine had already bought my plane tickets for Monday and had planned a welcome home party that evening. I know she was happy to have me coming home soon.

After returning back to the hostel, it was time for me to say goodbye to Joe. I went through my pack and took out all the stuff I wasn't going to need over the next week. I handed Joe my tent and took his rain tarp that he had brought with him. I wanted to make as much room in my pack as I could so I could take a solid five days of food with me into the 100 Mile Wilderness. I had an extra garbage bag in my pack and put all the extra gear in it to give to Joe so he could take it back with him. When we got everything packed up, we headed outside to the car.

We took a few pictures and said our goodbyes. I would see Mike and Ann Marie in exactly a week but it would be over a month before I saw Joe again as he would be in NJ working his summer job when I got home. The next time any of them would see me, I would be a thru-hiker. They wished me luck on getting to Katahdin and then climbed into the vehicle and pulled out of the driveway. I watched them drive down the road and turn the corner. I headed back into the house and went up to my room.

CHAPTER 17

100 Mile Wilderness

Unlike the times when Laine would leave after visiting me, watching Joe leave was much tougher. Normally when Laine would leave I would be hiking off into the woods. Being able to get back on the trail and hike north allowed me to clear my mind and work out the loneliness I would inevitably feel when leaving her behind. This time, I was stuck at a hostel and it was Father's Day. I felt an enormous wave of sadness come over me. I knew I needed to do something to take my mind off of feeling sad, so I decided to go and pick up some resupply at the General Store.

After getting some resupply, a cup of coffee, and returning back to the hostel, I started checking out the weather for the next week. We were scheduled to have thunderstorms and rain tomorrow, but the next five days after that would be sunny, followed by another rainy day. I really did not want to start off the wilderness getting wet, but it looked like there was nothing I could do about the weather. Talking to others at the hostel, there was an option to get dropped off about 15 miles north and that would allow me to hike back south to Rt. 15 and return to Shaw's for another night stay and, more importantly, an opportunity to dry out from the rain.

Speaking with Pizza Hut and Dragon, they were considering taking advantage of the opportunity to do the 15-mile day and returning to Shaw's. We finally all agreed we would do the 15 miles and spend one more night at Shaw's. It was a bit of a relief to know that I could get dried out tomorrow after getting wet. It would also allow me to get another good dinner and breakfast before entering the wilderness for good. After eating dinner, I tried to relax and just be prepared to get through the rain the next day. In the morning, I would be able to eat a big breakfast before heading out in the rain and I was really looking forward to it.

Shaw's was known for their breakfast and, for $9, it did not disappoint. Three eggs, any way you like them, bacon, and home fried potatoes. Add to that some coffee and if that was not enough, all-you-can-eat blueberry pancakes. Poet and Hippy Chick were the owners of the hostel and they ran a great place. There was a good crowd that spent the night as not only were there some NOBOs, but a wave of SOBOs were starting to get through the 100 Mile Wilderness and hit their first real trail town.

Dragon, Pizza Hut, and I ate our breakfast and then prepared to be shuttled 15 miles up the trail to hike south back to Shaw's. We loaded into Poet's SUV and he drove us to a logging road that had a trail connected to it. When we got out of the vehicle and got our packs on, Poet explained that we needed to follow the trail for about 8/10ths of a mile and it would intersect with the AT. We would then travel southbound for approximately 15 miles and end up back at Route 15. We told him we would see him later and headed on into the woods.

It was around 9 am when we started to hike and we were anxious to knock out these 15 miles and get back to the hostel at a decent time before the weather got too bad. It had already rained some overnight, so the roots and rocks were nice and slick. We moved quickly through the forest and got to the intersection with the AT within 20 minutes. All I kept thinking about was being able to get through the rain today and get back to the hostel. I kept my head down, watching the placement of my feet as I walked, looking up occasionally to make sure I was staying right behind Pizza Hut. A couple of hours into the hike, we stopped for a few minutes to eat a snack and drink some water but, for the most part, we just kept on hiking.

Several times throughout the morning and early afternoon we would hike through light rain showers but nothing too crazy. Before we knew it, we were eating up the miles and could start to see the light at the end of the tunnel. When we got about three miles from Route 15, the rain started to pick up and came down at a steady rate. The last mile or so we picked up the pace as the rain increased and so did the thunder and lightning. As I tried to move as fast as I could but also watch my footing, the thunder and lightning cracked around us. Being wet and carrying two metal poles in my hands while lightning filled the sky around me was not very comforting. I remember thinking to myself that it would really suck to make it this far, a hundred miles from the end, and get struck by lightning and die.

We came to a wooden bridge and as I tried to cross it, I felt my foot slip out from under me and down I went. Pizza Hut turned around to see if I was ok and I told him I was and picked myself up off the ground. We pushed on and finally rolled up to the trailhead at Route 15 a little after 3 pm. We called the hostel to let them know to send the shuttle and we waited for them to arrive. As we waited, I saw two hikers approaching from the trailhead on the opposite side of Route 15. I could see that it was a guy and a girl and as they got closer, I realized it was Peanut Butter and Jelly.

They joined us waiting for the shuttle and rode back with us to Shaw's. When we got back, I took off my wet clothes and had a nice hot shower. As I stood in the shower, I realized that it would be the last shower I would take on the trail. The next time I would shower would be after submitting Katahdin. The weather was looking good for the rest of the week with the exception of Sunday. Rain was supposed to start coming in on Saturday afternoon and continue through Sunday. I was approximately 100 miles from the end and had six days to get it done. Laine already had me plane tickets for Monday, so I had to be done by then.

After showering, I met a couple of new NOBOs that just arrived at the hostel. Shoemaker, a former Marine from New Hampshire, and Bullfrog from New Jersey. It was good to meet some more NOBOs since I had spent most of the second half of my hike alone, without seeing many NOBOs. With Dragon, Pizza Hut, Peanut Butter, and Jelly, there was a nice little group of NOBOs getting ready to make the final push.

After eating dinner and washing all my clothes for the last time, I packed my pack and tried to get some sleep. I had a big day tomorrow but was looking forward to starting the last section of this journey. My only concern was the weather on Sunday, the day I planned on summiting. For now, I could not worry about it. The next 30-40 miles had some climbs but then it would start to flatten out as we approached closer to Katahdin.

I ate another big breakfast the next morning and then gathered all of my stuff. As I was waiting for everyone else to get ready to start loading up the vehicles and head out to the trail, I was checking the weather again, hoping the weather for Sunday would get better. No such luck. We loaded into the SUV and headed back to the trail. As he drove, Poet started to tell us what we were about to encounter on the trail as far as the terrain was concerned. In 31 miles, we would climb White Cap Mountain, the highest peak in the 100 Mile Wilderness. More importantly, it would provide us with the first view of Mt. Katahdin.

Poet dropped us off back at the same spot he left us yesterday. Dragon, Pizza Hut, and I posed for a picture then headed back off into the woods. We followed the same spur trail and when we reached the connection to the AT, we turned the opposite way from yesterday and headed north. As we hiked, we were all focused on our own journey and really did not focus on each other. I had the Chairbacks to climb today and I spent the morning and part of the early afternoon climbing them. Pizza Hut and Dragon were ahead of me but I was not focused on keeping up with them. I stayed in my own thoughts and hiked my hike.

It was a long, hard day but the weather was nice. After climbing either up or down all day long, I came to the shelter a little after 7 pm. There were about five SOBOs already there and so was Dragon and Pizza Hut. I set up in the shelter and cooked and ate my dinner. As I got ready to go to bed, I studied my guidebook to plan out my day for tomorrow. I had four big climbs first thing in the morning but the fourth one was White Cap and I was really looking forward to that summit and setting my eyes on Katahdin for the very first time.

I was up early and on the trail by 6:15 am the next morning. I was anxious to get these four mountains out of the way as fast as I could today. While there would still be a few more mountains after them, the climbs would not be as big. It was a beautiful day and I expected to have a decent view of Katahdin when I got to White Cap. I climbed the first peak and then the next two. As I started White Cap, all I could think about was Katahdin.

Finally, I reached the summit of White Cap and took the very short spur trail to the east. As I walked out onto the rock cropping, I looked down on the rock and saw a white "K" spray painted on the rock with an arrow pointing straight ahead. As I followed the direction of the arrow and looked off into the sky, I could see it. After walking over 2100 miles in 142 days, I could see the mountain that I had thought about every day. I pulled out my Garmin and texted Laine, "I see Katahdin." I stood there for a moment staring at the mountain. I thought about how far I had come and for the first time, it really hit me that I was going to finish this hike. I could feel the emotion of the moment start to overcome me but I could also feel a strong desire to keep hiking and get to that mountain. After everything I had gone through over the last few months, the end was in sight

I took one final look and then returned back to the trail and started hiking. As I hiked, all I could think of was that mountain. The 100 Mile Wilderness was beautiful and I was enjoying just taking in all the sights and thinking about getting to the end. Eventually, I arrived at a shelter and stopped to eat some lunch. I had covered some pretty good mileage and it looked like the terrain in the afternoon was going to get flatter and hopefully a little easier. I started to think I could push a bigger day today and I looked in the guide to see what the camping options were going to be.

Since I started early this morning, I really was thinking I could push past the shelter I was going to stay at and go to a campsite that was almost 8 miles further. It would be the longest day of my entire journey but after seeing Katahdin, I was motivated to try it. I did not have phone service so I could not call Laine and tell her I was thinking of pushing further. I did have my Garmin but I did not want to make any promises to her in case I changed my mind. After a while, it really did not matter because Laine was tracking me on the computer and started to text me asking where I was headed. I replied that I did not know, I was going to keep hiking.

Finally, around 6 pm, I arrived at the Antler's Campsite and completed a 26.8-mile day. I felt great and was really excited about getting the extra miles in. Pizza Hut was already there and, to top it all off, I actually had some phone service at the campsite. It was Wednesday evening and I was only 46.5 miles away from Katahdin Stream Campground and the base of Mt. Katahdin. That meant that if I pushed it and did those miles in two days, I could summit on Saturday and miss the rain that was due later Saturday and Sunday.

I called Laine and told her there was a change of plans. I asked her to call Mike and Ann Marie and let them know that they could still plan on picking me up on Sunday, but I would meet them in Millinocket rather than them picking me up from Katahdin. I pulled out the tarp I took from Joe and set it up to sleep under. After eating some dinner and getting all set up, I retreated to my tarp as a light rain started to fall. I was camping right on the shore of Lower Jo-Mary Lake and I could hear the loons as the sun began to set.

The sun started to peek through the trees not long after an army of birds began their morning ritual of announcing the start of another day. I opened my eyes and peered towards the sun that was rising on the horizon. I was up and on the trail again before 6:30 am and was hiking with a purpose. Pizza Hut was still in his tent when I left but I figured I would see him later. I was looking to cover 25.5 miles today and that would set me up nicely to cover 21 miles the following day and be able to camp at the base of Katahdin and summit on Saturday.

Around noon, I made it to a shelter and stopped there for a 30-minute lunch break. I checked my mileage and had already clocked 13 miles and was a little over halfway to my goal for the day. I finished eating and was back to hiking in no time. I was able to catch a few more glimpses of Katahdin as I hiked and seeing the mountain get bigger and bigger as I got closer motivated me even more.

I reached Rainbow Spring campsite on the shores of Rainbow Lake a little after 5 pm and met a Boy Scout troop that was already at the campsite. I chatted with them for a few minutes before Pizza Hut arrived and we both found a spot closer to the shore of the lake to set up camp. We met a 75-year-old section hiker that was already set up near the shore and joined him. He had been section hiking the AT for years and was just a few hundred miles short of completing the entire thing. We talked and ate and then started to get ready to get some sleep.

As I laid down to go to sleep, I was excited to think that this would be the last night in the 100 Mile Wilderness and that I was about 36 hours away from finishing my hike. Tomorrow, I had 11 miles to hike to get to the end of the wilderness and get to Abol Campground Store and the restaurant that was there. My plan was to get there by lunch so that I could get a cheeseburger and then pick up a small resupply at the store to get me covered for the hike up Katahdin the next day. I would then hike 10 miles into Baxter State Park and camp at Katahdin Stream Campground. I had a big day ahead of me and I could not wait to get up in the morning.

The temperatures got down to 44 degrees overnight but with my 0-degree quilt, I was nice and warm and I slept really well. Waking up in the morning, I packed my stuff up and did my normal morning routine. As I was going through my morning ritual, I was constantly thinking about how the next time I woke up, I would be getting ready to summit Katahdin. It was hard to believe that my journey was about to come to an end. While part of me was excited and happy to see it end, the other part of me knew that I would miss being on the trail.

Pizza Hut headed out a few minutes before I did but I was still able to get going by 6:40 am. The restaurant was supposed to open at 11 am and I wanted to get there as close to opening time as possible. The trail was still full of roots and rocks but I just kept pushing forward. I ran into several SOBOs as I hiked and each one of them stopped to congratulate me on my upcoming summit. It was pretty cool to think back to my first few days on the trail when I saw a few SOBOs who were finishing up their hikes from the year before. There was a certain feeling of wanting to be in their position. Now I was and it felt great.

About 5-6 miles in for the morning, I made a short climb up to Rainbow Ledges where I had some good views of Katahdin.

It was a great place to stop for 5 minutes and have a snack and some water. I did a pretty good job on my last resupply as I entered the 100 Mile Wilderness with a big food bag but I had been eating more frequently. Most of my food was gone and that made my pack so much lighter. As much as I enjoyed looking at Katahdin, I was ready to get to Abol bridge.

As I pushed north, I kept thinking about the fact that, in 24 hours, I would be somewhere on Katahdin. I also started to think about the climb up Katahdin and wondered how tough it would be. I started to wonder if it would take me most of the day. At the Monson Visitor's Center, they told us that normal people take 10-12 hours to summit and return. For thru-hikers, it doesn't take that long but it was still something I had never done and as I got closer, I could hear the voices of doubt in my head. I reminded myself that I had hiked over 2100 miles and made it through the Whites and Southern Maine. Katahdin would be tough but I would make it, no matter what it took.

Finally, I came across the sign that was welcoming SOBOs into the 100 Mile Wilderness. I was at the northern end and I had completed the 100 Mile Wilderness. All that was left now was a short walk out of the woods and onto the road that would take me to Abol Bridge. As I emerged from the woods and turned onto Golden Road, I looked at my watch and it was just a few minutes before 11 am. Perfect timing. I approached Abol Bridge and as I started to cross it, I looked to my left and stopped dead in my tracks. Right there before my eyes, there she was in all her glory. The clear blue sky was the perfect backdrop for my close-up view of my goal. Staring back at me was the mighty Mt. Katahdin. There were no more mountains to climb between me and Katahdin and only a mere 10 miles of flat trail separated me from the final mountain.

CHAPTER 18

Baxter

At the end of the bridge was the Abol camp store and the restaurant. Sitting outside the restaurant was Pizza Hut waiting for me. As I approached, he stated, "it doesn't open until 11 am" and I looked at my watch and announced, "it is 11 am!" We walked into the restaurant and took a seat. A waitress came up to us and told us their computer was down and it would be a while until they would be up and running. We told her that was fine and decided to sit and wait until they were ready. After just a few minutes, the waitress returned and told us it would be at least two hours.

Realizing they were not really interested in trying to serve anyone anytime soon, we decided to go next door to the store and see what we could find. We were disappointed that we would not be able to get a burger, but at that point, we really did not care. After tomorrow, we could have whatever we wanted. We settled for expensive pre-made deli sandwiches from the camp store and picked up several other snacks and drinks to eat for lunch and to supplement whatever remaining items we had in our food bags. All we needed was enough to get us through to lunch tomorrow.

We took our food and plopped down on the ground outside of the restaurant to eat. As we sat and ate, we heard some familiar voices. I looked up to see Shoemaker and Bullfrog approaching the restaurant. I had a feeling I would see them before we got to Katahdin and I was right. As they arrived, I broke the news to them that the restaurant was not serving anyone for at least a couple of hours and the over-priced camp store snacks were their only option. We spoke for a minute and then they went inside the store to see what they could find.

Pizza Hut and I finished eating and, after a break, decided to get the last 10 miles done and get to camp. It was 12:30 pm when we started back hiking and we crossed over the boundary of Baxter State Park. Shortly after entering the park, we came across a kiosk and signed up on the kiosk to stay at the Birches, the shelter in the park that was reserved for northbound long-distance hikers that have at least completed the 100 Mile Wilderness. It only holds 12 people and when the list fills up, you have to find another camping option. It cost $10 per person to stay there which is payable at the Ranger Station at the Katahdin Stream Campsite in the park. Fortunately, no one else was on the list and Pizza Hut and I secured the first two spots.

We were able to hike the 10 miles to the Ranger Station in less than 3 1/2 hours and went inside to see the Ranger. We paid our $10 camping fee and registered to summit the next morning. He went over the rules and instructions for climbing Katahdin with us, then gave me my summit card and I was the #21 NOBO for the year. We left the office and took the short road walk to the Birches which included two small shelters, a privy, and a few wooded tent pads. We set up in one of the shelters and started to relax.

Not too long after getting settled in, Shoemaker and Bullfrog showed up and set up their hammock and tent. We ate some dinner and talked about getting this thing over with and getting to be back home. Pizza Hut still had to flip back down to Virginia and head south but he was about to complete the tougher northern section. After getting eaten up by some mosquitoes, Pizza Hut decided to put up his tent to keep them away. As for me, for whatever reason, the mosquitoes were leaving me alone so I was comfortable staying in the shelter.

We were all just relaxing and trying to pass the time until it got dark and we could officially go to sleep. There was a sense of anticipation and a desire for morning to arrive so we could get hiking. I reorganized the gear in my pack and tried to get everything ready for the morning. My plan was to wake up early and try to be hiking as soon as it got light outside. I did not know how long it would take me to hike, so I wanted to get going early.

As it started to get dark, I finished preparing my gear and laid down to get some sleep. It would be my last night on the trail and it was bittersweet. While I tried to go to sleep, it was difficult. Part of me was anxious to climb Katahdin as I did not know what to expect. I was also excited for the opportunity to close this thing out. Like a kid trying to go to sleep on Christmas Eve, I laid there while a million thoughts and emotions raced in my head. I set my alarm on my phone just to make sure I did not accidentally oversleep. Eventually, I drifted off. Throughout the night, I would wake up and look at my watch. I would then close my eyes again and try to fall back asleep, hoping the next time I woke up, it would be time to get up and get going.

Finally, at 4:23 am, I woke up and decided I would get up and start to pack my stuff. I took my time getting ready and it wasn't long before the others were up and getting packed up. Shoemaker and Bullfrog got ready and headed out. They were both ready to get the hike over with and get back to their homes in New Hampshire and New Jersey. When Pizza Hut and I were ready, we donned our packs and headed off to the Ranger Station. It was a short 5-minute walk and when we arrived, we left some of our stuff inside the porch of the Ranger Station and headed back out the door.

We walked up the dirt road from the Ranger Station and headed towards the Hunt Trail, the path that would take us to our destination on the top of Katahdin. The last stretch of trail on the AT is 5.2 miles long and starts out relatively easily. Pizza Hut led the way and I followed behind. I focused on staying right behind Pizza Hut and did not worry about anything else but moving forward. The climb up Katahdin would be one of the toughest, if not the toughest, on the entire Appalachian Trail. The mountain climbed 4100 feet over 5.2 miles and I knew that even though it was relatively easy at this point, it was going to get extremely tough very soon.

After a mile of hiking, we arrived at Katahdin Stream Falls. Stopping to look at the falls, I had a drink of water and knew that this was going to get difficult. As we got moving again, the trail began to climb at a steeper pace than before. As Pizza Hut used all of his tall and lanky gait to step on and over the roots and rocks that covered the trail, I tried to move my legs fast enough to keep up. We passed a set of day hikers that were on their way up the mountain and we kept pushing north. I was sweating a good bit but I did not seem to care. I was down to my last few miles on the trail. I would look up occasionally to make sure I was maintaining my pace with Pizza Hut and then just keep pushing.

The trail was full of rocks and roots but, by now, I had become used to dealing with them. At this point in my trek, nothing was going to keep me from getting to the top. As I climbed, I looked up towards the treetops and tried to gauge how much longer I had until I would climb above tree line. As I continued upward, the forest got brighter and brighter until the trees started to thin out and I began to catch a glimpse of a view between the trees.

Eventually, I climbed out of the wood line and was greeted with nothing but granite and some of the most beautiful views

Glenn Justis

I had seen the entire trip. We both stopped to take in the views of the 100 Mile Wilderness and all of the ponds that littered the landscape. I took some pictures and had a drink of water. In front of us was nothing but the granite face of Katahdin with the occasional white blaze painted on it. We carefully maneuvered our way around, up, and over the rocks. At times, there would be rebar embedded into the granite so as to provide a foothold or handhold to grab onto and pull yourself up.

We stopped again for a few moments to take some more pictures and drink some more water. We could see the false summit that leads to the tablelands and I knew we were getting close. Staring upward, all I could see was a carpet of granite stones covering the ground before me. The occasional white blaze was painted on the rocks, and as I reached one, I would look for the next one to hike towards. Eventually, we reached the tablelands and got to some reasonably flat terrain. The ground was still covered with granite rocks but at least there was a short break from having to climb. The tablelands stretched about a mile and then the trail would turn upward for the last 800 feet to climb.

I pulled out my phone to take some pictures and stared across the Tablelands at the final climb of the entire Appalachian Trail. The scene reminded me of a moonscape and being there felt like no other mountain I had been on since starting my trek. I tried to take it all in and I thought back to not only the journey I took to get here, but also thought back to when I first decided to make this hike. I was one mile from Baxter Peak and the end of the AT. The difficult part of the climb was over and I tried to take in the moment. The weather was beautiful and I thanked God for protecting me and for giving me a spectacular day to summit.

The trail turned towards the left and the final climb. As we approached, I saw two hikers were heading towards us from the summit. As they got closer, I could see it was Shoemaker and Bullfrog. They were overjoyed with emotion as they approached us and gave us a fist bump and words of encouragement. They had been to the summit and were heading back down the mountain. Pizza Hut and I were next.

I thought about that cold day on Springer Mountain and the feeling I had when I said goodbye to Laine and Joe and walked off into the woods alone. I thought about having to leave Laine again at Fontana Dam. I remembered the moment I heard about Cotter passing and all the snow we hiked through. I remembered the trip home for Cotter's memorial service and the return back to the trail. I remembered the last time I said goodbye to Laine in New Jersey and hiking with Joe in Maine. Despite the difficult times, I remembered the people that I met along the way. Not only the trail angels but also the hostel and hotel owners. Above all, I remembered the hikers. From the first section hikers I spent the night with on Day 1 to all the thru-hikers I hiked with for a day, or in the case of Fun Size and Old Soul, several weeks. It was a lifetime of experiences rolled into 145 days.

Closing in on the summit, I could start to make out the famous sign sitting alone on the peak. I saw the sign from a distance and I could feel the emotions start to build. For some reason, it felt like the sign appeared too soon. I felt this couldn't be the end. It seemed to appear sooner than it should have. I wanted this moment to move in slow motion but my legs would not let that happen. My adrenaline was pumping and every part of my body was wanting to get to the sign I had thought about every single day, since Georgia. I could see that a couple of day hikers were at the summit, so I slowed down so that Pizza Hut would have time to summit and I would have a few moments to savor the last few steps of my journey.

I pumped my legs and drove myself forward as I planted my trekking poles into the ground. I maneuvered around the rocks that littered the landscape, carefully weaving my way to the summit. Stepping from rock to rock and would look up every other step or so to check how close I was getting to the summit. Pizza Hut and a couple of day hikers were already at the summit, standing well in front of the sign to allow plenty of room for me to get to the sign. The brown sandwich board sign grew larger and larger as I took each step. Finally, I took my last few steps and found myself face to face with the finish line.

I looked at Pizza Hut and flashed a thumbs up before dropping to my knees in front of the sign and bowing my head. I thanked God for keeping me safe the entire way and thanked all my trail angels in heaven who gave me the strength to keep going when things got their toughest.

A wave of relief came over me and I stood back up and stared at the infamous sign. At that moment, I looked around me and tried to take it all in. I was at the end of a trail that started 2,190.9 miles to the south. I had traversed 14 states and climbed up and over hundreds of mountains. Despite the cold, snow, rain, heat and every other form of weather that was thrown at me, I kept moving forward. During my hike, I fell 78 times but picked myself up each time and continued forward. I traveled every mile of the trail and I did it all by foot power.

Before I could call Laine, I received a congratulatory text

from my friend and Assistant Scoutmaster, Mark, who had been following my trek on Garmin. I sent a quick response to him and then was able to get a quick phone call out to Laine to let her know I had reached the summit. I looked at my watch and the time was 8:40 am. It took us just a little over 2 1/2 hours to summit. Pizza Hut and I hung out on the summit having a snack and trying to take it all in. The wind was starting to pick up pretty good and I could see the sky slowly filling with clouds. There was possible rain called for later in the afternoon but, at this point, I did not care about what the weather was going to do. For the first time in 145 days, I did not need to check the weather.

After taking a good 30-minute break on the summit, Pizza Hut and I decided to start heading back down to the Ranger's station so we could pick up the rest of our stuff and try to get a ride into Millinocket. The trek was over. I was a thru-hiker.

CHAPTER 19

The Trail Provides

Hiking the trail was definitely the hardest thing I have ever done in my life. As with most difficult challenges in life, the trail provided me with more benefits than I could ever imagine. By the time I reached the sign at the top of Baxter Peak, I was ready to be done. I was looking forward to climbing down the mountain and getting back to my family and friends. My body was tired but it had served me well. My feet were swollen and they had been that way for months. I lost 50 lbs and my current weight was 138 lbs. While my body was physically beat up, I felt strong - physically, mentally, and emotionally.

Despite the time away from home and loved ones, despite the hardships I faced along the way, I walked every step of the trail and accomplished my goal. I learned I could be as tough as I needed to be regardless of what the trail or life could throw at me. The trail, much like life, is not something you conquer, it is something you endure. If not for the suffering during the hard times along the way, I would not have been able to enjoy all the good times. I am a different person now compared to when I started.

When I first decided to start this journey, I encountered a wide variety of opinions about what I was about to do. Most were positive but I know there were some who privately did not understand why I would want to leave the life I had and walk 2,200 miles. I learned over the course of the hike that we cannot live our lives worrying about other people's opinions of our lives and our choices. I also learned a lot of other important things.

On the trail, people do not judge each other. We are all hikers and that is all that matters. I find it quite interesting that town or city life is known as "civilization" but people often do not act very civilized. On the trail, people are friendly and are always willing to help each other out. No one judges you. It doesn't matter what you do or did for a living, what age you are, or what nationality or race you are. People are people. In "civilization" these days, we are constantly bombarded by advertisers who tell us how our lives won't be satisfying if we don't have their products or services. Our society has turned into one of consumption and that has led to people becoming self-absorbed and less caring about the simple things in life.

On the trail, I had to carry everything I needed to survive on my back. I learned that I did not need much to survive. In fact, I did not need much to be happy. My diet consisted of some basic food. Nothing gourmet for me. I was happy if there was a Dollar General store that I could resupply in when I stopped in town. Eating a bowl of Ramen noodles with some tuna was something I looked forward to at the end of a long day of hiking, especially when I was wet and cold.

I learned how to be comfortable being alone. Hiking for 10-12 hours a day, mostly all alone, provided me with one very important gift. The ability to complete a thought. I had time to think and time to think through a situation. Back in civilization, we never get the time to fully complete a thought. We are constantly interrupted by a number of distractions. We live in an age where we are constantly expected to be "plugged in" and available to others 24 hours a day. We have "working" lunches and cannot even enjoy time with family without having to check our phones for messages. Being away from all of those distractions was an amazing experience.

I also learned a lot about the relationships I have in my life. While I have always loved my wife and son, the absence from them just made that love stronger. I could hardly wait to get home and be with them again. Hiking the trail also revealed a lot about my friendships. Throughout one's life, you meet a lot of people and you make a lot of friends. Most of the people you meet in life are really just acquaintances. They are people you spend time with because you happen to work together, live near each other, or have some other common interests. Then, there are friends.

Friends are the people that care for you and love you for who you really are and not who they want you to be. They will be there for you when times are tough and your spirits are low. They sacrifice their own well-being for you. The trail helped me to see who my real friends were. There were some who I thought were my friends and they were not. When I hit the trail, the communication with them stopped. They turned their backs on me when I was no longer beneficial to them. I learned that I did not need them in my life and could spend the time I normally would spend on them with others who did want to spend time with me. There were others, however, that I never considered to be a close friend. They showed me more support and friendship than I could ask for during my hike. Old friends I had not seen or spoken to in years, reappeared in my life and supported me throughout my hike. Sometimes it was a simple text message to check in on me or a few words of encouragement on a Facebook or Instagram post. The trail brought them back to me.

The trail angels I met along the way were amazing. They would sacrifice their time and money to help total strangers by providing food, drink, a ride, or even a place to lay our heads. They cannot begin to understand the appreciation a hiker feels when they are the recipient of this trail magic. As I made my way along the trail, I was the recipient of a tremendous amount of trail magic. Every time I received some magic, it was something that I was in need of at that very moment. It is hard to hike the entire trail without getting a sense that there is a power greater than us who is watching over us and guiding others to help us when we are in a time of need.

Since returning from the trail, I have had some opportunities to do trail magic for other hikers. Being able to provide a small amount of comfort to them is an incredible feeling. Having been the recipient of trail magic, I fully appreciate the act of trail magic and I understand the tremendous gift you are giving someone when you bring them a cold drink, a hot meal, or a warm bed. The simple act of giving someone a hitch into town is a gift of enormous benefit to a hiker. The trail provides. It provides the hiker with the opportunity to humble themselves and accept the help and it provides the angel with the feeling of love and kindness that helping a total stranger provides.

After spending 11 years as a Criminal Prosecutor, I had the opportunity to handle thousands of cases and got to see some of the worst that human nature has to offer. Prosecuting murderers, child molesters, drug dealers, and a variety of other individuals had made me jaded. While I enjoyed my job and loved doing what I did, it was nice to remove myself from that world and have an opportunity to re-evaluate things.

I learned that I don't want to be remembered for what I did for a living. While I was proud of the accomplishments I was able to achieve in my career, those accomplishments pale in comparison with the true success stories of my life. A job or career is first and foremost a way to earn money so that we may do the things we truly want to do in life. In most cases, people put too much emphasis on their jobs and careers. We are all replaceable in the eyes of our employers. We are expected to show loyalty to our employers, yet loyalty is not shown to us. It does not matter how long you have worked somewhere or how well you have performed, everyone can and will be replaced when your existence is no longer beneficial to those for whom you work.

For several years before deciding to thru-hike, I thought about leaving my job and starting my own solo-law practice. While I enjoyed being a prosecutor, low morale and a lack of leadership in the office had really started to affect the office as a whole. As the culture began to get worse, I knew I had to do something. It was at this point that I decided to take some time off and clear my thoughts. Doing this thru-hike was exactly what I needed to do.

As I hiked and met more and more people, the conversation would inevitably turn to what the person did for a living. I found myself and others spending less and less time talking about their jobs and more time talking about their families and all the other experiences they had enjoyed in their lives. It became more apparent each day that a career does not have to define who a person is or how successful their lives had been.

For years, I dedicated myself to my career and my job. I put in extra hours at the office and tried to handle more cases than anyone else. Whenever I was asked to do something, I took on the extra responsibility and did the best that I could. I never backed down from a challenge and expected others to conduct themselves the same way. What I learned, however, is that being a hard worker is not enough. In fact, it is not even required. That wasn't who I was and it wasn't who I wanted to be.

For me, my time volunteering as a Scout leader was much more important than putting criminals away for a living. Being able to have a small impact on the lives of a young scout was what mattered the most. Seeing other scouts get to experience things for the first time and seeing them push themselves to accomplish things they did not know they could accomplish was worth more to me than gold. As I hiked up every mountain, I would think of the scouts back home who were following me. There was no way in hell I was going to quit knowing that others were expecting me to finish.

Above all, I learned that life is short and life is finite. Prior to hiking the trail, I lost both my parents and one of my brothers. We are not guaranteed tomorrow and we should never take it for granted. If there are things you want to do, you need to do them as soon as possible. When I lost one of my scouts while I was on the trail, the lesson could not have been driven home more effectively. You must live in the present and appreciate all that God has given you. After Cotter's death, I would be constantly reminded of his presence. From the sighting of an Eagle flying high above me, to the song of a White-Throated Sparrow as I would arrive above tree line on another arduous climb in New England. He was with me and he was letting me know that everything would be ok.

When I met and spoke with section hikers, I could see in them the person I was before starting the trail. They loved hiking and they loved all that the trail had to offer, but they felt trapped in their day to day lives. They had jobs, kids, a spouse, bills, and all the other reasons hikers give when they tell you they would like to thru-hike but cannot do it at this time. They would tell me they plan on doing the whole trail when they retire. They asked me how I was able to do it and convince my wife. I told them everything changed when I stopped telling myself all the reasons I could not do it now and I started asking myself how I could do it now.

Growing up, I constantly heard my Dad talk about things that he wanted to do. He used to tell us he wanted to buy a sailboat, he wanted to visit California, and many other things. When my Dad passed away in 2012 and my Mom passed away just 5 months later, they were both in South Carolina and their bodies had to be flown back to New Jersey for burial. That was the first time either one of them had been on an airplane. They were married for 55 years and raised three good sons. Despite that, I wondered if they were able to do all the things they ever dreamed of in their lives.

I was blessed to be raised by two wonderful parents and had two awesome brothers. Looking back at my decision to attend The Citadel, I realize it was one of the best decisions I have made in my life. It taught me the value of perseverance and helped to instill in me a sense of duty to others. The people I met while attending the school became more than just friends to me. They became brothers.

The trail provides each hiker with what they need most. When I started my hike, I was convinced that I would not stay in shelters and only use them when absolutely necessary. Not long into my hike, I started using the shelters and continued to do so throughout. The trail taught me who my true friends were and who just pretended to be my friend. The trail has taught me how to accept new things and not be so rigid in my thinking. The trail taught me to slow down.

When I left for the trail, I had a summit date already planned. As I would learn, the trail does not always conform to what we want. Throughout my hike, I would look at my mileage and compare it to where I thought I needed to be in order to summit when I wanted to summit. I had it all planned out that I would summit a week before I actually did and that Joe would hike the 100 Mile Wilderness with me and summit with me. The trail had other plans. It was not until I was sitting all alone at Speck Pond Shelter, taking what would be my last zero-day, that I finally realized that the trail was telling me to slow down. Up to that point, I was pushing to try to get done by a certain date. As I sat in the shelter with the rain and wind blowing outside, I finally allowed myself to slow down.

The four nights that I spent at Pine Ellis Hostel before meeting up with Joe in Rangeley were some of the best days on the trail. I finally gave myself permission to slow down and enjoy where I was and how far I had come. It was exactly what I needed after nearly 2,000 miles on the trail. All that I needed to do was stop and listen to what the trail was trying to tell me. The trail, like life, will help to show us what we really need if we will just give it a chance and listen to what it is telling us.

Above all, I learned that I am a lucky man. I have a wonderful wife, who is not only my spouse but my best

friend. Despite all my faults, and there are many, she has never let me down. No one on this earth knows the struggles I faced on the trail. Through it all, she was there and supported me in every way conceivable. Along with Laine, I had the support and love of my son, Joe. I missed him terribly and was so happy to see him when I emerged from the woods in Rangeley and knew that, for the next nine days, we would hike together. The trail knew what I needed at that time and it provided it.

The love and support I received from Laine, Joe, and the many friends and relatives along the way was much stronger than any of the mountains and rocks I encountered along the way. They were my rocks and they were tougher than granite. There was never a doubt that I would make it to the end but I could never predict the experiences I had along the way. As I sit here and write these words, I cannot help but wonder how long it will be before I pack up my backpack and hit the trail again. The trail has taught me so much and despite the hardships and the desire to get it over with and get back home, it calls out to me. The trail is part of me. I have left too much on the trail not to return. Anyone who has spent time on the trail understands its power. For those who have not experienced it, I encourage you to do so. We all travel a different path on the same trail. They say it never leaves you and I hope to God it never leaves me. As long as I remain on this Earth, I will always remember the time I spent walking to Maine.

Made in the USA
Columbia, SC
04 May 2020